FOR THE SAKE OF THE SCHOOL

ANGELA BRAZIL

For the Sake of the School

Angela Brazil

© 1st World Library, 2007
PO Box 2211
Fairfield, IA 52556
www.1stworldlibrary.com
First Edition

LCCN: 2007930719

Softcover ISBN: 978-1-4218-4793-1
Hardcover ISBN: 978-1-4218-4696-5
eBook ISBN: 978-1-4218-4890-7

Purchase *"For the Sake of the School"*
as a traditional bound book at:
www.1stWorldLibrary.com/purchase.asp?ISBN=978-1-4218-4793-1

1st World Library is a literary, educational organization
dedicated to:

- Creating a free internet library of downloadable ebooks

- Hosting writing competitions and offering book publishing
scholarships.

Interested in more 1st World Library books? contact:
literacy@1stworldlibrary.com
Check us out at: www.1stworldlibrary.com

1st World Library Literary Society

Giving Back to the World

"If you want to work on the core problem, it's early school literacy."

- James Barksdale, former CEO of Netscape

"No skill is more crucial to the future of a child, or to a democratic and prosperous society, than literacy."

- Los Angeles Times

"Literacy... means far more than learning how to read and write... The aim is to transmit... knowledge and promote social participation."

- UNESCO

"Literacy is not a luxury, it is a right and a responsibility. If our world is to meet the challenges of the twenty-first century we must harness the energy and creativity of all our citizens."

- President Bill Clinton

"Parents should be encouraged to read to their children, and teachers should be equipped with all available techniques for teaching literacy, so the varying needs and capacities of individual kids can be taken into account."

- Hugh Mackay

TO THE SCHOOLGIRL READERS WHO HAVE
SENT ME SUCH NICE LETTERS

CONTENTS

CHAPTER I

THE WOODLANDS

"Are they never going to turn up?"

"It's almost four now!"

"They'll be left till the six-thirty!"

"Oh, don't alarm yourself! The valley train always waits for the express."

"It's coming in now!"

"Oh, good, so it is!"

"Late by twenty minutes exactly!"

"Stand back there!" yelled a porter, setting down a box with a slam, and motioning the excited, fluttering group of girls to a position of greater safety than the extreme edge of the platform. "Llangarmon Junction! Change for Glanafon and Graigwen!"

Snorting and puffing, as if in agitated apology for the tardiness of its arrival, the train came steaming into the station, the drag of its brakes adding yet another item of noise to the prevailing babel. Intending passengers clutched bags and baskets; fathers of families gave a last eye to the luggage; mothers grasped children firmly by the hand; a distracted youth, seeking vainly for his portmanteau, upset a stack of bicycles with a crash; while above all the din and turmoil rose the strident, rasping voice of a book-stall boy, crying his selection of papers with ear-splitting zeal.

From the windows of the in-coming express waved seventeen agitated pocket-handkerchiefs, and the signal was answered by a counter-display of cambric from the twenty girls hustled back by an inspector in the direction of the weighing-machine.

"There's Helen!"

"And Ruth, surely!"

"Oh! where's Marjorie?"

"There! Can't you see her, with Doris?"

"That's Mamie, waving to me!"

"What's become of Kathleen?"

One moment more, and the neat school hats of the new-comers had swelled the group of similar school hats already collected on the platform; ecstatic greetings were exchanged, urgent questions asked and hasty answers given, and items of choice information poured forth with the utmost volubility of which the English tongue is capable. Urged by brief directions from a mistress in charge, the chattering crew surged towards a siding, and made for a particular corridor carriage marked "Reserved". Here handbags, umbrellas, wraps, and lunch-baskets were hastily stowed away in the racks, and, Miss Moseley having assured herself that not a single lamb of her flock was left behind, the grinning porter slammed the doors, the green flag waved, and the local train, long overdue, started with a jerk for the Craigwen Valley.

Past the grey old castle that looked seawards over the estuary, past the little white town of Llangarmon, with its ancient walls and fortified gates, past the quay where the fishing smacks were lying idly at anchor and a pleasure-steamer was unloading its human cargo, past the long stretch of sandy common, where the white tents of the Territorials evoked an outcry of interest, then up alongside the broad tidal river towards where the mountains, faint and misty, rose shouldering one another till they merged into the white nebulous region of the cloud-flecked sky. Those lucky ones who had secured window seats on the river side of the carriage were loud in their acclamations of satisfaction as familiar objects in the landscape came into sight.

"There's Cwm Dinas. I wish they could float a big Union Jack on the summit."

"It would be a landmark all right."

"Oh, the flag's up at Plas Cafn!"

"We'll have one at school this term?"

"Oh, I say! Move a scrap," pleaded Ulyth Stanton plaintively. "We only get fields and woods on our side. I can't see anything at all for your heads. You might move. What selfish pigs you are! Well, I don't care; I'm going to talk."

"You have been talking already. You've never stopped, in fact," remarked Beth Broadway, proffering a swiftly disappearing packet of pear drops with a generosity born of the knowledge that all sweets would be confiscated on arrival at The Woodlands.

"I know I have, but that was merely by the way. It wasn't anything very particular, and I've got something I want to tell you—something fearfully important. Absolutely super! D'you know, she's actually coming to school. Isn't it great? She's to be my room-mate. I'm just wild to see her. I hope her ship won't be stopped by storms."

"By the Muses, whom are you talking about?"

"'She' means the cat," sniggered Gertrude Oliver.

"Why! can't you guess? What stupids you are! It's Rona, of course—Rona Mitchell from New Zealand."

"You're ragging!"

"It's a fact. It is indeed!"

The incredulity on the countenances of her companions having yielded to an expression of interest, Ulyth continued her information with increased zest, and a conscious though would-be nonchalant air of importance.

"Her father wants her to go to school in England, so he decided to send her to The Woodlands, so that she might be with me!"

"Do you mean that girl you were so very proud of corresponding with? I forget how the whole business began," broke in Stephanie Radford.

"Don't you remember? It was through a magazine we take.

The editor arranged for readers of the magazine in England to exchange letters with other readers overseas. He gave me Rona. We've been writing to each other every month for two years."

"I had an Australian, but she wouldn't write regularly, so we dropped it," volunteered Beth Broadway. "I believe Gertrude had somebody too."

"Yes, a girl in Canada. I never got farther than one short letter and a picture post card, though. I do so loathe writing," sighed Gertrude. "Ulyth's the only one who's kept the thing up."

"And do you mean to say this New Zealander's actually coming to our school?" asked Stephanie.

"That's the joysome gist of my remarks! I can't tell you how I'm pining and yearning to see her. She seems like a girl out of a story. To think of it! Rona Mitchell at school with us!"

"Suppose you don't like her?"

"Oh, I'm certain I shall! She's written me the jolliest, loveliest, funniest letters! I feel I know her already. We shall be the very best of friends. Her father has a huge farm of I can't tell you how many miles, and she has two horses of her own, and fords rivers when she's out riding."

"When's she to arrive?"

"Probably to-morrow. She's travelling by the *King George*, and coming up straight from London to school directly she lands. I hope she's got to England safely. She must have left home ever such a long time ago. How fearfully exciting for her to—"

But here Ulyth's reflections were brought to an abrupt close, for the train was approaching Glanafon Ferry, and her comrades, busily collecting their various handbags, would lend no further ear to her remarks.

The little wayside station, erstwhile the quietest and sleepiest on the line, was soon overflowing with girls and their belongings. Miss Moseley flitted up and down the platform, marshalling her charges like a faithful collie, the one porter did his slow best, and after a few agitated returns to the compartments for forgotten articles, everything was successfully collected, and the train went steaming away down the valley in the direction of Craigwen. It seemed to take the last link of civilization with it, and to leave only the pure, unsullied country behind. The girls crossed the line and walked through the white station gate with pleased anticipation writ large on their faces. It was the cult at The Woodlands to idolize nature and the picturesque, and they had reached a part of their journey which was a particular source of pride to the school.

Any admirer of scenery would have been struck with the lovely and romantic view which burst upon the eye as the travellers left the platform at Glanafon and walked down the short, grassy road that led to the ferry. To the south stretched the wide pool of the river, blue as the heaven above where it caught the reflection of the September sky, but dark and mysterious where it mirrored the thick woods that shaded its banks. Near at hand towered the tall, heather-crowned crag of Cwm Dinas, while the rugged peaks of Penllwyd and Penglaslyn frowned in majesty of clouds beyond. The ferry itself was one of those delightful survivals of mediaevalism which linger here and there in a few fortunate corners of our isles. A large flat-bottomed boat was slung on chains which spanned the river, and could be worked slowly across the water by means of a small windlass. Though it was perfectly possible, and often even more convenient, to drive to the school direct from Llangarmon Junction, so great was the popular feeling in favour of arrival by the ferry that at the autumn and spring reunions the girls were allowed to avail themselves of the branch railway and approach The Woodlands by way of the river.

They now hurried on to the boat as if anticipating a pleasure-jaunt. The capacities of the flat were designed to accommodate a flock of sheep or a farm wagon and horses, so there was room and to spare even for thirty-seven girls and their hand luggage. Evan Davis, the crusty old ferryman, greeted them with his usual inarticulate grunt, a kind of "Oh, here you are again, are you!" form of welcome which was more forceful than gracious. He linked the protecting chains carefully across the end of the boat, called out a remark in Welsh to his son, Griffith, and, seizing the handle, began to work the windlass. Very slowly and leisurely the flat swung out into the river. The tide was at the full and the wide expanse of water seemed like a lake. The clanking chains brought up bunches of seaweed and river grass which fell with an oozy thud upon the deck. The mountain air, blowing straight from Penllwyd, was tinged with ozone from the tide. The girls stood looking up the reach of water towards the hills, and tasting the salt on their lips with supreme gratification. It was not every school that assembled by such a romantic means of conveyance as an ancient flat-bottomed ferry-boat, and they rejoiced over their privileges.

"I'm glad the tide's full; it makes the crossing so much wider," murmured Helen Cooper, with an eye of admiration on the woods.

"Don't suppose Evan shares your enthusiasm," laughed Marjorie Earnshaw. "He's paid the same, whatever the length of the journey."

"Old Grumps gets half a crown for his job, so he needn't grumble," put in Doris Deane.

"Oh, trust him! He'd look sour at a pound note."

"What makes him so cross?"

"Oh, he's old and lame, I suppose, and has a crotchety temper."

"Here we are at last!"

The boat was grating on the shore. Griffith was unfastening the movable end, and in another moment the girls were springing out gingerly, one by one, on to the decidedly muddy stepping-stones that formed a rough causeway to the bank. A cart was waiting to convey the handbags (all boxes had been sent as "advance luggage" two days before), so, disencumbered of their numerous possessions, the girls started to walk the steep uphill mile that led to The Woodlands.

Miss Bowes and Miss Teddington, the partners who owned the school, had been exceptionally fortunate in their choice of a house. If, as runs the modern theory, beautiful surroundings in our early youth are of the utmost importance in training our perceptions and aiding the growth of our higher selves, then surely nowhere in the British Isles could a more suitable setting have been found for a home of education. The long terrace commanded a view of the whole of the Craigwen Valley, an expanse of about sixteen miles. The river, like a silver ribbon, wound through woods and marshland till it widened into a broad tidal estuary as it neared the sea. The mountains, which rose tier after tier from the level green meadows, had their lower slopes thickly clothed with pines and larches; but where they towered above the level of a thousand feet the forest growth gave way

Angela Brazil

to gorse and bracken, and their jagged summits, bare of all vegetation save a few clumps of coarse grass, showed a splintered, weather-worn outline against the sky. Penllwyd, Penglaslyn, and Glyder Garmon, those lofty peaks like three strong Welsh giants, seemed to guard the entrance to the enchanted valley, and to keep it a place apart, a last fortress of nature, a sanctuary for birds and flowers, a paradise of green shade and leaping waters, and a breathing-space for body and soul.

The house, named "The Woodlands" by Miss Bowes in place of its older but rather unpronounceable name of Llwyngwrydd (the green grove), took both its Welsh and English appellations from a beautiful glade, planted with oaks, which formed the southern boundary of the property. Through this park-like dell flowed a mountain stream, tumbling in little white cascades between the big boulders that formed its bed, and pouring in quite a waterfall over a ledge of rock into a wide pool. Its steady rippling murmur never stopped, and could be heard day and night through the ever-open windows, gentle and subdued in dry weather, but rising to a roar when rain in the hills brought the flood down in a turbulent torrent.

Through lessons, play, or dreams this sound of many waters was ever present; it gave an atmosphere to the school which, if passed unnoticed through extreme familiarity, would have been instantly missed if it could have stopped. To the girls this stream was a kind of guardian deity, with the glade for its sacred grove. They loved every rock and stone and cataract, almost every patch of brown moss upon its boulders. Each morning of the summer term they bathed before breakfast in the pool where a big oak-tree shaded the cataract. It was so close to the house that they could run out in mackintoshes, and so retired that it resembled a private swimming-bath. Here they enjoyed themselves like water-nymphs, splashing in the shallows, plunging in the pool, swinging from the boughs of the oak-tree, and scrambling over the lichened boulders. It was a source of deep regret to the hardier spirits that they were not allowed to take their morning dip in the stream all the year round; but on that score mistresses were adamant, and with the close of September the naiads perforce withdrew from their favourite element till it was warmed again by the May sunshine.

The house itself had originally been an ancient Welsh dwelling of the days of the Tudors, but had been largely added to in later times. The straight front, with its rows of windows, classic doorway, and stone-balustraded terrace, was certainly Georgian in type, and the tower, an architectural eyesore, was plainly Victorian. The taste of the early nineteenth century had not been faultless, and all the best part of the building, from an artistic point of view, lay at the back. This mainly consisted of kitchens and servants' quarters, but there still remained a large hall, which was the chief glory of the establishment. It was very lofty, for in common with other specimens of the period it had no upper story, the roof being timbered like that of a church. The walls were panelled with oak to a height of about eight feet, and above that were decorated with elaborate designs in plaster relief, representing lions, wild boars, stags, unicorns, and other heraldic devices from the coat-of-arms of the original owner of the estate. A narrow winding staircase led to a minstrels' gallery, from which was suspended a wooden shield emblazoned with the Welsh dragon and the national motto, "Cymru am byth" ("Wales for ever").

If the hall was the main picturesque asset of the building, it must be admitted that the unromantic front portion was highly convenient, and had been most readily adaptable for a school. The large light rooms of the ground floor made excellent classrooms, and the upper story was so lavishly provided with windows that it had been possible, by means of wooden partitions, to turn the great bedrooms into rows of small dormitories, each capable of accommodating two girls.

The bright airy house, the terrace with its glorious view of the valley, the large old-fashioned garden, and, above all, the stream and the glade made a very pleasant setting for the school life of the forty-eight pupils at The Woodlands. The two principals worked together in perfect harmony. Each had her own department. Miss Bowes, who was short, stout, grey-haired, and motherly, looked after the housekeeping, the hygiene, and the business side. She wrote letters to parents, kept the accounts, interviewed tradespeople, superintended the mending, and was the final referee in all matters pertaining to health and general conduct. "Dear Old Rainbow", as the girls nicknamed her, was frankly popular, for she was sympathetic and usually disposed to listen, in reason, to the various plaints which were brought to the sanctum of her private sitting-room. Her authority alone could excuse preparation, order breakfast in bed, remit practising, dispense jujubes, allow special festivities, and grant half-holidays. It was rumoured that she thought of retiring and leaving the school to her partner, and such a report always drew from parents the opinion that she would be greatly missed.

Miss Teddington, younger by many years, took a more active part in the teaching, and superintended the games and outdoor sports. She was tall and athletic, a good mathematician, and interested in archaeology and nature study. She led the walks and rambles, taught the Sixth Form, and represented the more scholastic and modern element. Her enterprise initiated all fresh undertakings, and her enthusiasm carried them forward with success. "Hard-as-nails" the girls sometimes called her, for she coddled nobody and expected the utmost from each one's capacity. If she was rather uncompromising, however, she was just, and a strong vein of humour toned down much of the severity of her remarks. To be chided by a person whose eye is capable of twinkling takes part of the sting from the reprimand, and the general verdict of the school was to the effect that "Teddie was a keen old watch-dog, but her bark was worse than her bite."

Of the other mistresses and girls we will say more anon. Having introduced my readers to The Woodlands, it is time for the story to begin.

CHAPTER II

A FRIEND FROM THE BUSH

Ulyth Stanton was a decided personality in the Lower Fifth. If not exactly pretty, she was a dainty little damsel, and knew how to make the best of herself. Her fair hair was glossy and waved in the most becoming fashion, her clothes were well cut, her gloves and shoes immaculate. She had an artistic temperament, and loved to be surrounded by pretty things. She was rather a favourite at The Woodlands, for she had few sharp angles and possessed a fair share of tact. If the girls laughed sometimes at what they called her "high-falutin' notions" they nevertheless respected her opinions and admired her more than they always chose to admit. It was an accepted fact that Ulyth stuck to her word and generally carried through anything that she once undertook. She alone of six members of her form who had begun to correspond with girls abroad, at the instigation of the magazine editor, had written regularly, and had cultivated the overseas friendship with enthusiasm. The element of romance about the affair had appealed to Ulyth. It was so strange to receive letters from someone you had never seen. To be sure, Rona had only given a somewhat bald account of her home and her doings, but even this outline was so different from English life that Ulyth's imagination filled the gaps, and pictured her unknown correspondent among scenes of unrivalled interest and excitement. Ulyth had once seen a most wonderful film entitled "Rose of the Wilderness", and though the scenes depicted were supposed to be in the region of the Wild West, she decided that they would equally well represent the backwoods of New Zealand, and that the beautiful, dashing, daring heroine, so aptly called "the Prairie Flower", was probably a speaking likeness of Rona Mitchell. When she learnt that owing to her letters Rona's father had determined to send his daughter to school at The Woodlands, her excitement was immense. She had at once petitioned Miss Bowes to have her as a room-mate, and was now awaiting her advent with the very keenest anticipation.

There was a little uncertainty about the time of the new girl's arrival, for it depended upon the punctuality of the ocean liner, a doubtful matter if there were a storm; and the feeling that she might be expected any hour between 9 a.m. and 4 p.m. made havoc of Ulyth's day. It was impossible to attend to lessons when she was listening for the sound of a taxi on the drive, and even the attractions of tennis could not decoy her out of sight of the front door.

"I must be the very first to welcome her," she persisted. "Of course it's not the same to all the rest of you—I understand that. She's to be my special property, my Prairie Rose!"

"All serene! If you care to waste your time lounging about the steps you can. We're not in such a frantic state to see your paragon," laughed the girls as they ran down the garden to the courts. After all, the waiting was in vain. Tea-time came without a sign of the new-comer. It was unlikely that she would turn up now until the evening train, and Ulyth resigned herself to the inevitable. But when the school was almost half-way through its bread and butter and gooseberry jam, a sudden commotion occurred in the hall. There was a noise such as nobody ever remembered to have heard at The

Angela Brazil

Woodlands before.

"Thank goodness gracious I've got meself here at last!" cried a loud nasal voice. "Where'll I stick these things? Oh yes, there's heaps more inside that automobile! Travelling's no joke, I can tell you; I'm tired to death. Any tea about? I could drink the sea. My gracious, I've had a time of it coming here!"

At the first word Miss Bowes had glided from the room, and the voice died away as the door of her private study closed. Sounds suggestive of the carrying upstairs of luggage followed, and a hinnying laugh echoed once down the stairs. The girls looked at one another; there was a shadow in Ulyth's eyes. She did not share in the general smile that passed round the table, and she finished her tea in dead silence.

"Going to sample your new property?" whispered Mary Acton as the girls pushed back their chairs.

"What's the formula for swearing an undying friendship?" giggled Addie Knighton.

"Was it Rose of Sharon you called her?" twinkled Christine Crosswood. "Or Lily of the Valley?"

Ulyth did not reply. She walked upstairs very slowly. The nasal twang of that high-pitched voice in the hall had wiped the bloom off her anticipation. The small double dormitory in which she slept was No. 3, Room 5. The door was half-open, so she entered without knocking. Both beds, the chairs, and most of the floor was strewn with an assortment of miscellaneous articles. On the dressing-table was a tray with the remains of tea. Over a large cabin trunk bent a girl of fourteen. She straightened herself as she heard footsteps.

Alas! alas! for Ulyth's illusions. The enchanting vision of the prairie flower faded, and Rona Mitchell stood before her in solid fact. Solid was the word for it—no fascinating cinema heroine this, but an ordinary, well-grown, decidedly plump damsel with brown elf locks, a ruddy sunburnt complexion, and a freckled nose.

Where, oh, where, were the delicate features, the fairy-like figure, and the long rich clustering curls of Rose of the Wilderness? Ulyth stood for a moment gazing as one dazed; then, with an effort, she remembered her manners and introduced herself.

"Proud to meet you at last," replied the new-comer heartily. "You and I've had a friendship switched on for us ready-made, so to speak. I liked your letters awfully. Glad they've put us in together."

"Did—did you have a nice journey?" stammered Ulyth.

It was a most conventional enquiry, but the only thing she could think of to say.

"Beastly! It was rough or hot all the time, and we didn't get much fun on board. Wasn't it a sell? Too disappointing for words! Mrs. Perkins, the lady who had charge of me coming over, was just a Tartar. Nothing I did seemed to suit her somehow. I bet she was glad to see the last of me. Then I was sea-sick, and when we got into the hot zone—my, how bad I was! My face was just skinned with sunburn, and the salt air made it worse. I'd not go to sea again for pleasure, I can tell you. I say, I'll be glad to get my things fixed up here."

"This is your bed and your side of the room," returned Ulyth hastily, collecting some of the articles which had been flung

Angela Brazil

anywhere, and hanging them in Rona's wardrobe; "Miss Moseley makes us be very tidy. She'll be coming round this evening to inspect."

Rona whistled.

"Guess she'll drop on me pretty often then! No one's ever called neatness my strong point. Are those photos on the mantelpiece your home folks? I'm going to look at them. What a lot of things you've got: books, and albums, and goodness knows what! I'll enjoy turning them over when I've time."

At half-past eight that night a few members of the Lower Fifth, putting away books in their classroom, stopped to compare notes.

"Well, what do you think of your adorable one, Ulyth?" asked Stephanie Radford, a little spitefully. "You're welcome to her company so far as I'm concerned."

"Rose of the Wilderness, indeed!" mocked Merle Denham.

"Your prairie rose is nothing but a dandelion!" remarked Christine Crosswood.

"I never heard anyone with such an awful laugh," said Lizzie Lonsdale.

"Don't!" implored Ulyth tragically. "I've had the shock of my life. She's—oh, she's too terrible for words! Her voice makes me cringe. And she pawed all my things. She snatched up my photos, and turned over my books with sticky fingers; she even opened my drawers and peeped inside."

"What cheek!"

"Oh, she hasn't the slightest idea of how to behave herself! She asked me a whole string of the most impertinent questions: what I'd paid for my clothes, and how long they'd have to last me. She's unbearable. Yes, absolutely impossible. Ugh! and I've got to sleep in the same room with her to-night."

"Poor martyr, it's hard luck," sympathized Lizzie. "Why did you write and ask the Rainbow to put you together? It was rather buying a pig in a poke, wasn't it?"

"I never dreamt she'd be like this. It sounded so romantic, you see, living on a huge farm, and having two horses to ride. I shall go to Miss Bowes, first thing to-morrow morning, and ask to have her moved out of my room. I only wish there was time to do it this evening. Oh, why did I ever write to her and make her want to come to this school?"

"Poor old Ulyth! You've certainly let yourself in for more than you bargained for," laughed the girls, half sorry for her and half amused.

Next morning, after breakfast, the very instant that Miss Bowes was installed in her study, a "rap-tap-tap" sounded on her door.

"Come in!" she called, and sighed as Ulyth entered, for she had a shrewd suspicion of what she was about to hear.

"Please, Miss Bowes, I'm sorry to have to ask a favour, but may Rona be changed into another dormitory?"

"Why, Ulyth, you wrote to me specially and asked if you might have her for a room-mate!"

"Yes, I did; but I hadn't seen her then. I thought she'd be

Angela Brazil

so different."

"Isn't it a little too soon to judge? You haven't known her twenty-four hours yet."

"I know as much of her as I ever want to. Oh, Miss Bowes, she's dreadful! I'll never like her. I can't have her in my room—I simply can't!"

There was a shake, suggestive of tears, in Ulyth's voice. Her eyes looked heavy, as if she had not slept. Miss Bowes sighed again.

"Rona mayn't be exactly what you imagined, but you must remember in what different circumstances she has been brought up. I think she has many good qualities, and that she'll soon improve. Now let us look at the matter from her point of view. You have been writing to her constantly for two years. She has come here specially to be near you. You are her only friend in a new and strange country where she is many thousand miles away from her own home. You gave her a cordial invitation to England, and now, because she does not happen to realize your quite unfounded expectations, you want to back out of all your obligations to her. I thought you were a girl, Ulyth, who kept her promises."

Ulyth fingered the corner of the tablecloth nervously for a moment, then she burst out:

"I can't, Miss Bowes, I simply can't. If you knew how she grates upon me! Oh, it's too much! I'd rather have a bear cub or a monkey for a room-mate! Please, please don't make us stop together! If you won't move her, move me! I'd sleep in an attic if I could have it to myself."

"You must stay where you are until the end of the week. You

owe that to Rona, at any rate. Afterwards I shall not force you, but leave it to your own good feeling. I want you to think over what I have been saying. You can come on Sunday morning and tell me your decision."

"I know what the answer will be," murmured Ulyth, as she went from the room.

She was very angry with Miss Bowes, with Rona, and with herself for her own folly.

"It's ridiculous to expect me to take up this savage," she argued. "And too bad of Miss Bowes to make out that I'm breaking my word. Oh dear! what am I to write home to Mother? How can I tell her? I believe I'll just send her a picture post card, and only say Rona has come, and no more. Miss Bowes has no right to coerce me. I'll make my own friends. No, I've quite made up my mind she shan't cram Rona down my throat. To have that awful girl eternally in my bedroom—I should die!"

After all her heroics it was a terrible come-down for poor Ulyth now the actual had taken the place of the sentimental. Her class-mates could not forbear teasing her a little. It was too bad of them; but then they had resented her entire pre-appropriation of the new-comer, and, moreover, had one or two old scores from last term to pay off. Ulyth began to detest the very name of "the Prairie Flower". She wondered how she could ever have been so silly.

"I ought to have been warned," she thought, trying to throw the blame on to somebody else. "No one ever suggested she'd be like this. The editor of the magazine really shouldn't have persuaded us to write. It's all his fault in the beginning."

Though the rest of the girls were scarcely impressed with

Angela Brazil

Rona's personality, they were not utterly repelled.

"She's rather pretty," ventured Lizzie Lonsdale. "Her eyes are the bluest I've ever seen."

"And her teeth are so white and even," added Beth Broadway. "She looks jolly when she smiles."

"Perhaps she'll smarten up soon," suggested Addie Knighton. "That blue dress suits her; it just matches her eyes."

To Ulyth's fastidious taste Rona's clothes looked hopelessly ill-cut and colonial, especially as her room-mate put them on anyhow, and seemed to have no regard at all for appearances. A girl who did not mind whether she looked really trim, spruce and smart, must indeed have spent her life in the backwoods.

"Didn't you even have a governess in New Zealand?" she ventured one day. She did not encourage Rona to talk, but for once her curiosity overcame her dislike of the high-pitched voice.

"Couldn't get one to stop up-country, where we were. Mrs. Barker, our cowman's wife, looked after me ever since Mother died. She was the only woman about the place. One of our farm helps taught me lessons. He was a B.A. of Oxford, but down on his luck. Dad said I'd seem queer to English girls. I don't know that I care."

Though Rona might not be possessed of the most delicate perceptions, she nevertheless had common sense enough to realize that Ulyth did not receive her with enthusiasm.

"I suppose you're disappointed in me?" she queried. "Dad said you would be, but I laughed at him. Pity if our ready-made friendship turned out a misfit! I think you're no end! Dad said I'd got to copy you; it'll take me all my time, I expect. Things are so different here from home."

Was there a suspicion of a choke in the words?

Ulyth had a sudden pang of compunction. Unwelcome as her companion was to her, she did not wish to be brutal.

"You mustn't get home-sick," she said hastily. "You'll shake down here in time. Everyone finds things strange at school just at first. I did myself."

"I guess you were never as much a fish out of water as me, though," returned Rona, and went whistling down the passage.

Ulyth tried to dismiss her from her thoughts. She did not intend to worry over Rona more than she could possibly help. Fortunately they were not together in class, for Rona's entrance-examination papers had not reached the standard of the Lower Fifth, and she had been placed in IV B.

Ulyth was interested in her school-work. She stood well with her teachers, and was an acknowledged force in her form. She came from a very refined and cultured home, where intellectual interests were cultivated both by father and mother. Her temperament was naturally artistic; she was an omnivorous reader, and could devour anything in the shape of literature that came her way. The bookcase in her dormitory was filled with beautiful volumes, mostly Christmas and birthday gifts. She rejoiced in their soft leather bindings or fine illustrations with a true book-lover's enthusiasm. It was her pride to keep them in daintiest condition. Dog-ears or thumb-marks were in her opinion the depths of degradation. Ulyth had ambitions also, ambitions which she would not reveal to anybody. Some day she planned to write a book of her own. She had not yet fixed on a subject, but she had decided just what the cover was to be like, with her name on it in gilt letters. Perhaps she might even illustrate it herself, for her love of art almost equalled her love of literature; but that was still in the clouds, and must wait till she had chosen her plot. In the interim she wrote verses and short stories for the school magazine, and her essays for Miss Teddington were generally returned marked "highly creditable".

This term Ulyth intended to study hard. It was a promotion to be in the Upper School; she was beginning several new subjects, and her interest in many things was aroused. It would be a delightful autumn as soon as she had got rid of this dreadful problem, at present the one serious obstacle to her comfort. But in the meantime it was only Friday, and till at least the following Monday she would be obliged to endure her uncongenial presence in her bedroom.

CHAPTER III

ROUND THE CAMP-FIRE

It was the first Saturday of the term. So far the girls had been kept busily occupied settling down to work in their fresh forms, and trying to grow accustomed to Miss Teddington's new time-tables. Now, however, they were free to relax and enjoy themselves in any way they chose. Some were playing tennis, some had gone for a walk with Miss Moseley, a few were squatting frog-like on boulders in the midst of the stream, and others strolled under the trees in the grove.

"Thank goodness the weather's behaving itself!" said Mary Acton, who, with a few other members of the Lower Fifth, was sitting on the trunk of a fallen oak. "Do you remember last council? It simply poured. The thing's no fun if one can't have a real fire."

"It'll burn first-rate to-night," returned Lizzie Lonsdale. "There's a little wind, and the wood'll be dry."

"That reminds me I haven't found my faggot yet," said Beth Broadway easily.

"Girl alive! Then you'd better go and look for one, or you'll be all in a scramble at the last!"

Angela Brazil

"Bother! I'm too comfy to move."

"Nice Wood-gatherer you'll look if you come empty-handed!"

"I'd appropriate half your lot first, Lizzikins!"

"Would you, indeed? I'd denounce you, and you'd lose your rank and be degraded to a candidate again."

"Oh, you mean, stingy miser!"

"Not at all. It's the wise and foolish virgins over again. I shan't have enough for myself and you. I've a lovely little stack—just enough for one—reposing—no, I'd better not tell you where. Don't look so hopeful. You're not to be trusted."

"What are you talking about?" asked Rona Mitchell, who had wandered up to the group. "Why are some of you picking up sticks? I saw a girl over there with quite a bundle just now. You might tell me."

So far Rona had not been well received in her own form, IV B. She was older than her class-mates, and they, instead of attempting to initiate her into the ways of the Woodlands girls on this holiday afternoon, had scuttled off and left her to fend for herself. She looked such an odd, wistful, lonely figure that Lizzie Lonsdale's kind heart smote her. She pushed the other girls farther along the tree-trunk till they made a grudging space for the new-comer.

"I'm a good hand at camp-fires, if you want any help," continued Rona, seating herself with alacrity. "I've made 'em by the dozen at home, and cooked by them too. Just let me know where you want it, and I'll set to work."

"You wouldn't be allowed," said Beth bluntly. "This fire is a very special thing. Only Wood-gatherers may bring the fuel. No one else is eligible."

"Why on earth not?"

"Oh, I can't bother to explain now! It would take too long. You'll find out to-night. Girls, I'm going in!"

"Turn up here at dusk if you want to know, and bring a cup with you," suggested Lizzie, with a half-ashamed effort at friendliness, as she followed her chums.

"You bet I'll turn up! Rather!"

That evening, just after sunset, little groups of girls began to collect round an open green space in the glade. They came quietly and with a certain sense of discipline. A stranger would have noticed that if any loud tone or undue hilarity made itself heard, it was instantly and firmly repressed by one or two who seemed in authority. That the meeting was more in the nature of a convention than a mere pleasure-gathering was evident both from the demeanour of the assemblage and from the various badges pinned on the girls' coats. No teacher was present, but there was an air of general expectancy, as if the coming of somebody were awaited. To the pupils at The Woodlands this night's ceremony was a very special occasion, for it was the autumn reunion of the Camp-fire League, an organization which, originally of American birth, had been introduced at the instigation of Miss Teddington, and had taken great root in the school. Any girl was eligible as a candidate, but before she could gain admission to even the initial rank she had to prove herself worthy of the honour of membership, and pass successfully through her novitiate.

The organizer and leader of the branch which to-night was to celebrate its third anniversary was a certain Mrs. Arnold, a charming young American lady who lived in the neighbourhood. She had been an enthusiastic supporter of the League in Pennsylvania before her marriage, and was delighted to pass on its traditions to British schoolgirls. Her winsome personality made her a prime favourite at The Woodlands, where her influence was stronger even than she imagined. Miss Teddington, though it was she who had asked Mrs. Arnold to institute and take charge of the meetings, had the discretion to keep out of the League herself, realizing that the presence of teachers might be a restraint, and that the management was better left in the hands of a trustworthy outsider.

To become an authorized Camp-fire member was an ambition with most of the girls, and spurred many on to greater efforts than they would otherwise have attempted. All looked forward to the meetings, and there could be no greater punishment for certain offences than a temporary withdrawal of League privileges.

This September, after the long summer holiday, the reunion seemed of even more than ordinary importance.

The sun had set, the last gleam of the afterglow had faded, and the glade had grown full of dim shadows by the time everybody was present in the grove. The gentle rustle of the leafy boughs overhead, and the persistent tumbling rush of the stream, seemed like a faint orchestral accompaniment of Nature for the ceremonial.

"Is it a Quakers' Meeting or a Freemasons' Lodge? You're all very mum," asked Rona, whom curiosity had led out with the others.

"Sh-sh! We're waiting for our 'Guardian of the Fire'," returned Ulyth, trying to suppress the loudness of the high-pitched voice. "Mrs. Arnold's generally very punctual. Oh, there! I believe I hear her ringing her bicycle bell now. I'm going down the field to meet her."

Ulyth regarded Mrs. Arnold with that intense adoration which a girl of fifteen often bestows on a woman older than herself. She ran now through the wood, hoping she might be in time to catch her idol on the drive and have just a few precious moments with her before she was joined by the others. There were many things she wanted to pour into her friend's ready ears, but she knew it would be impossible to monopolize her as soon as the rest of the girls knew of her arrival. She fled as on wings, therefore, and had the supreme satisfaction of being the first in the field. Mrs. Arnold, young, very fair, graceful, and golden-haired, looked a picture in her blue cycling costume as she leaned her machine against a tree and greeted her enthusiastic admirer.

"Oh, you darling! I've such heaps to tell you!" began Ulyth, clasping her tightly by the arm. "Rona Mitchell has come, and she's the most awful creature! I never was so disappointed in my life. Don't you sympathize with me, when I expected her to be so ripping? She's absolute backwoods!"

"Yes, I've heard all about her. Poor child! She must have had a strange training. It's time indeed she began to learn something."

"She's not learned anything in New Zealand. Oh, her voice will just grate on you! And her manners! She's hopeless! Everything she does and says is wrong. And to think she's been foisted on to me, of all people!"

"Poor child!" repeated Mrs. Arnold. ("Which of us does she

mean?" thought Ulyth.) "She's evidently raw material. Every diamond needs polishing. What an opportunity for a Torch-bearer!"

Ulyth dropped her friend's arm suddenly. It was not at all the answer she had expected. Moreover, at least a dozen girls had come running up and were claiming their chief's attention. In a species of triumphant procession Mrs. Arnold was escorted into the glade and installed on her throne of state, a seat made of logs and decorated with ferns. Everyone clustered round to welcome her, and for the moment she was the centre of an enthusiastic crowd. Ulyth followed more slowly. She was feeling disturbed and put out. What did Mrs. Arnold mean? Surely not—? A sudden thought had flashed into her mind but she thrust it away indignantly. Oh no, that was quite impossible! It was outrageous of anybody to make the suggestion. And yet—and yet—the uneasy voice that had been haunting her for the last four days began to speak with even more vehemence. With a sigh of relief she heard the signal given for "Attention", and cast the matter away from her for the moment. Every eye was fixed on their leader. The ceremony was about to begin.

Mrs. Arnold rose, and in her clear, sweet voice proclaimed:

"The Guardian of the Fire calls on the Wood-gatherers to bring their fuel."

At once a dozen girls came forward, each dragging a tolerably large bundle of brushwood. They deposited these in a circle, saluted, and retired.

"Fire-makers, do your work!" commanded the leader.

Eight girls responded, Ulyth among the number, and seizing the brushwood, they built it deftly into a pile. All stood round, waiting in silence while their chief struck a match and applied a light to some dried leaves and bracken that had been placed beneath. The flame rose up like a scarlet ribbon, and in a few moments the dry fuel was ablaze and crackling. The gleam lighting up the glade displayed a picturesque scene. The boles of the trees might have been the pillars in some ancient temple, with the branches for roof. Close by the cascade of the stream leapt white against a background of dim darkness. The harvest moon, full and golden, was rising behind the crest of Cwm Dinas. An owl flew hooting from the wood higher up the glen. Mrs. Arnold stood waiting until the bonfire was well alight, then she turned to the expectant girls.

"I've no need to tell most of you why we have met here to-night; but for the benefit of a few who are new-comers to The Woodlands I should like briefly to explain the objects of the Camp-fire League. The purpose of the organization is to show that the common things of daily life are the chief means of beauty, romance, and adventure, to cultivate the outdoor habit, and to help girls to serve the community—the larger home—as well as the individual home. In these ultra-modern times we must especially devote ourselves to the service of the country, and try by every means in our power to make our League of some national use. First let us repeat together the rules of the Camp-fire League:

"'1. Seek beauty.
2. Give service.
3. Pursue knowledge.
4. Be trustworthy.
5. Hold on to health.
6. Glorify work.
7. Be happy.'"

"Seeking beauty includes more than looking for superficial

adornment. Beauty is in all life, in Nature, in people, in the love of one's heart, in virtue and a radiant disposition. The value of service depends largely upon the attitude of mind of the one rendering it. Joy in the performance of some needed service in behalf of parent, teacher, friend, or country constitutes a part of the very essence of goodness, and multiplies the good already abiding in the heart. This is the third anniversary of the founding of a branch of the League at The Woodlands. So far the work has been very encouraging, and I am glad to say that to-night we have candidates eligible for all three ranks. It shall now be the business of the meeting formally to admit them. Candidates for Wood-gatherers, present yourselves!"

Six of the younger girls came forward and saluted.

"Can you repeat, and will you promise to obey, the seven rules of the Camp-fire law?"

Each responded audibly in the affirmative.

"Then you are admitted to the initial rank of Wood-gatherers, you are awarded the white badge of service, and may sign your names as accepted members of the League."

The six retired to make way for a higher grade, and eight other girls stepped into the firelight.

"Candidates for Fire-makers, you have passed three months with good characters as Wood-gatherers, and you have proved your ability to render first aid, keep accounts, tie knots, and prepare and serve a simple meal; you have each committed to memory some good poem, and have acquainted yourself with the career of some able, public-spirited woman. Having thus shown your wish to serve the community, repeat the Fire-maker's desire."

And all together the eight girls chanted:

"As fuel is brought to the fire
So I purpose to bring
My strength,
My ambition,
My heart's desire,
My joy,
And my sorrow
To the fire
Of human kind.
For I will tend
As my fathers have tended
And my fathers' fathers
Since time began,
The fire that is called
The love of man for man,
The love of man for God."

Mrs. Arnold said a few kind words to each as she pinned on their red badges. Only novices who had stood the various tests with credit were raised to the honour of the second rank. Those who had failed must perforce continue as Wood-gatherers for another period of three months.

There remained one further and higher rank, only attainable after six months' ardent and trustworthy service as Fire-makers. To-night three girls were to be admitted to its privileges, and Helen Cooper, Doris Deane, and Ulyth Stanton presented themselves. With grave faces they repeated the Torch-bearer's desire:

"That light which has been given to me I desire to pass undimmed to others."

Ulyth kissed Mrs. Arnold's pretty hand as the long-coveted

yellow badge was fastened on to her dress, side by side with the Union Jack. She was so glad to be a Torch-bearer at last. She had become a candidate when the League was first founded three years ago, and all that time she had been slowly working towards the desired end of the third rank. One or two slips had hindered her progress, but last term she had made a very special effort, and it was sweet to meet with her reward. Torch-bearers were mostly to be found among the Sixth and Upper Fifth; she was the only girl in V B who had won so high a place. She touched the yellow ribbon tenderly. It meant so much to her.

Now that the serious business of the meeting was over, the fun was about to begin. The big camp-kettle was produced and filled at the stream, and then set to boil upon the embers. Cups and spoons made their appearance. Cocoa and biscuits were to be the order of the evening, followed by as many songs, dances, and games as time permitted. Squatting on the grass, the girls made a circle round their council-fire. Marjorie Earnshaw, one of the Sixth, had brought her guitar, and struck the strings every now and then as an earnest of the music she intended to bring from it later on. Everybody was in a jolly mood, and inclined to laugh at any pun, however feeble. Mrs. Arnold, always bright and animated, surpassed herself, and waxed so amusing that the circle grew almost hysterical. The Wood-gatherers, whose office it was to mix the cocoa, supplied cup after cup, and refilled the kettle so often that they ventured to air the time-honoured joke that the stream would run dry, for which ancient chestnut they were pelted with pebbles.

When at last nobody could even pretend to be thirsty any longer, the cups were rinsed in the pool and stacked under a tree, and the concert commenced. Part-songs and catches sounded delightful in the open air, and solos, sung to the accompaniment of Marjorie's guitar, were equally effective.

The girls roared the choruses to popular national ditties, and special favourites were repeated again and again. Several step-dances were executed, and had a weird effect in the unsteady light of the waning fire. Mrs. Arnold, who was a splendid elocutionist, gave a recitation on an incident in the American War, and was enthusiastically encored. The moon had risen high in the sky, and was peeping through the tree-tops as if curious to see who had invaded so sylvan a spot as the glade. The silver beams caught the ripples of the stream and made the shadows seem all the darker.

It was a glorious beginning for the new term, as everybody agreed, and an earnest of the fun that was in store later on.

"We shan't be able to camp out next meeting, but we'll have high jinks in the hall," purred Beth Broadway.

"Yes; Mrs. Arnold says she has a lovely programme for the winter, and we're to have candles instead of fuel," agreed Lizzie Lonsdale, who had been raised that evening to the rank of Fire-maker.

"Trust Mrs. Arnold to find something new for us to do!" murmured Ulyth, looking fondly in the direction of her ideal.

"My gracious, I call this meeting no end!" piped a cheerful voice in her ear; and Rona, smiling with all-too-obtrusive friendliness, plumped down by her side. "You've good times here, and no mistake! I think I'll be a candidate myself next, if that's the game to play. You're a high-and-mighty one, aren't you? Let's have a look at your badge!"

"If you dare to touch it!" flared Ulyth, putting up her hand to guard her cherished token.

"Why, I wouldn't do it any harm, I promise you; I wouldn't

finger it! It means something, doesn't it? I didn't quite catch what it was. You might tell me. How'm I ever to get to know if you won't?"

Rona's clear blue eyes, unconsciously wistful, looked straight into Ulyth's. The latter sprang to her feet without a word. The force of her own motto seemed suddenly to be revealed to her. She rushed away into the shadow of the trees to think it over for herself.

"That light which has been given to me I desire to pass undimmed to others."

Those were the words she had repeated so earnestly less than an hour ago. And she was already about to make them a mockery! Yes, that was what Mrs. Arnold had meant. She had known it all the time, but she would not acknowledge it even to her innermost heart. Was this what was required from a Torch-bearer—to pass on her own refinement and culture to a girl whose crudities offended every particle of her fastidious taste? Ulyth sat down on a stone and wept hot, bitter, rebellious tears. She understood only too well why she had been so miserable for the last three days. She had disliked Miss Bowes for hinting that she was not keeping her word, and had told herself that she was a much-tried and ill-used person.

"I must do it, I must, or fail at the very beginning!" she sobbed. "I know what Mother would say. It's got to be; if for nothing else, for the sake of the school. A Torch-bearer mustn't shirk and break her pledge. Oh, how I shall loathe it, hate it! Ulyth Stanton, do you realize what you're under-taking? Your whole term's going to be spoilt."

The big bell in the tower was clanging its summons to return, with short, impatient strokes. Everybody joined hands in a circle round the ashes of the camp-fire, to sing in a low chant the good-night song of the League and "God Save the Queen". Mr. Arnold, who had come to fetch his wife, was sounding his hooter as a signal on the drive. The evening's fun was over. Regretfully the girls collected cups, spoons, and kettle, and made their way back to the house.

On Sunday morning Ulyth, with a very red face, marched into the study, and announced:

"Miss Bowes, I've been having a tussle. One-half of me said: 'Don't have Rona in your room at any price!' and the other half said: 'Let her stop!' I've decided to keep her."

"I knew you would, when you'd thought it over," beamed Miss Bowes.

"Are all New Zealanders the same?" asked Ulyth. "I've not met one before."

"Certainly not. Most of them are quite as cultured and up-to-date as ourselves. There are splendid schools in New Zealand, and excellent opportunities for study of every kind. Poor Rona, unfortunately, has had to live on a farm far away from civilization, and her education and welfare in every respect seem to have been utterly neglected. Don't take her as a type of New Zealand! But she'll soon improve if we're all prepared to help her. I'm glad you're ready to be her real friend."

"I'll try my best!" sighed Ulyth.

Angela Brazil

CHAPTER IV

A BLACKBERRY FORAY

Having made up her mind to accept the responsibility which fate, through the agency of the magazine editor, had thrust upon her, Ulyth, metaphorically speaking, set her teeth, and began to take Rona seriously in hand. Being ten months older than her protegee, in a higher form, and, moreover, armed with full authority from Miss Bowes, she assumed command of the bedroom, and tried to regulate the chaos that reigned on her comrade's side of it. Rona submitted with an air of amused good nature to have her clothes arranged in order in her drawers, her shoes put away in the cupboard, and her toilet articles allotted places on her washstand and dressing-table. She even consented to give some thought to her personal appearance, and borrowed Ulyth's new manicure set.

"You're mighty particular," she objected. "What does it all matter? Miss Bowes gave me such a talking-to, and said I'd got to do exactly what you told me; and before I came, Dad rubbed it into me to copy you for all I was worth, so I suppose I'll have to try. I guess you'll find it a job to civilize me though." And her eyes twinkled.

Ulyth thought, with a mental sigh, that she probably would

find it "a job".

"No one bothered about it at home," Rona continued cheerfully. "Dad did say sometimes I was growing up a savage, but Mrs. Barker never cared. She let me do what I liked, so long as I didn't trouble her. She was no lady! We couldn't get a lady to stay at our out-of-the-way block. Dad used to be a swell in England once, but that was before I was born."

Ulyth began to understand, and her disgust changed to a profound pity. A motherless girl who had run wild in the backwoods, her father probably out all day, her only female guide a woman of the backwoods, whose manners were presumably of the roughest—this had been Rona's training. No wonder she lacked polish!

"When I compare her home with my home and my lovely mother," thought Ulyth, "yes—there's certainly a vast amount to be passed on."

The other girls, who had never expected her to keep Rona in her bedroom, were inclined to poke fun at the proceeding.

"Your bear cub will need training before you teach her to dance," said Stephanie Radford tauntingly.

"She has no parlour tricks at present," sniggered Addie Knighton.

"Are you posing as Valentine and Orson?" laughed Gertie Oliver. Gertrude had been Ulyth's room-mate last term, and felt aggrieved to be superseded.

"I call her the cuckoo," said Mary Acton. "Do you remember the young one we found last spring, sprawling all over the

Angela Brazil

nest, and opening its huge, gaping beak?"

In spite of her ignorance and angularities there was a certain charm about the new-comer. When the sunburn caused by her sea-voyage had yielded to a course of treatment, it left her with a complexion which put even that of Stephanie Radford, the acknowledged school beauty, in the shade. The coral tinge in Rona's cheeks was, as Doris Deane enviously remarked, "almost too good to look natural", and her blue eyes with the big pupils and the little dark rims round the iris shone like twinkling stars when she laughed. That ninnying laugh, to be sure, was still somewhat offensive, but she was trying to moderate it, and only when she forgot did it break out to scandalize the refined atmosphere of The Woodlands; the small white even teeth which it displayed, and two conspicuous dimples, almost atoned for it. The brown hair was brushed and waved and its consequent state of new glossiness was a very distinct improvement on the former elf locks. In the sunshine it took tones of warm burnt sienna, like the hair of the Madonna in certain of Titian's great pictures. Lessons, alack! were uphill work. Rona was naturally bright, but some subjects she had never touched before, and in others she was hopelessly backward. The general feeling in the school was that "The Cuckoo", as they nicknamed her, was an experiment, and no one could guess exactly what she would grow into.

"She's like one of those queer beasties we dug up under the yew-tree last autumn," suggested Merle Denham. "Those wriggling transparent things, I mean. Don't you remember? We kept them in a box, and didn't know whether they'd turn out moths, or butterflies, or earwigs, or woodlice!"

"They turned into cockchafer beetles, as a matter of fact," said Ulyth drily.

"Well, they were horrid enough in all conscience. I don't like Nature study when it means hoarding up creepy-crawlies."

"You're not obliged to take it."

"I don't this year. I've got Harmony down on my time-table instead."

"You'll miss the rambles with Teddie."

"I don't care. I'll play basket-ball instead."

"How about the blackberry foray?"

"Oh, I'm not going to be left out of that! It's not specially Nature study. I've put my name down with Miss Moseley's party."

The inmates of The Woodlands were fond of jam. It was supplied to them liberally, and they consumed large quantities of it at tea-time. To help to meet this demand, blackberrying expeditions were organized during the last weeks of September, and the whole school turned out in relays to pick fruit. A dozen girls and a mistress generally composed a party, which was not confined to any particular form, but might include any whose arrangements for practising or special lessons allowed them to go. Dates and particulars of the various rambles planned, with the names of the mistresses who were to be leaders, were pinned up on the notice-board, and the girls might put their names to them as they liked, so long as each list did not exceed twelve.

On Saturday afternoon Miss Moseley headed a foray in the direction of Porth Powys Falls, and Merle, Ulyth, Rona, Addie, and Stephanie were members of her flock.

"I'm glad I managed to get into this party," announced Merle, "because I always like Porth Powys better than Pontvoelas or Aberceiriog. It's a jollier walk, and the blackberries are bigger and better. I was the very last on the list, so I'd luck. Alice had to go under Teddie's wing. I'd rather have Mosie than Teddie!"

"So would I," agreed Ulyth. "I scribbled my name the very first of all. Just got a chance to do it as I was going to my music-lesson, before everyone else made a rush for the board. Porth Powys will be looking no end to-day."

Swinging their baskets, the girls began to climb a narrow path which ran alongside the stream up the glen. Some of them were tempted to linger, and began to gather what blackberries could be found; but Miss Moseley had different plans.

"Come along! It's ridiculous to waste our labour here," she exclaimed. "All these bushes have been well picked over already. We'll walk straight on till we come to the lane near the ruined cottage, then we shall get a harvest and fill our baskets in a third of the time. Quick march!"

There was sense in her remarks, so Merle abandoned several half-ripe specimens for which she had been reaching and joined the file that was winding, Indian fashion, up the path through the wood. Over a high, ladder-like stile they climbed, then dropped down into the gorge to where a small wooden bridge spanned the stream. They loved to stand here looking at the brown rushing water that swirled below. The thick trees made a green parlour, and the continual moisture had carpeted the woods with beautiful verdant moss which grew in close sheets over the rocks. Up again, by an even steeper and craggier track, they climbed the farther bank of the gorge, and came out at last on to the broad hill-side that overlooked the Craigwen Valley.

Here was scope for a leader; the track was so overgrown as to be almost indistinguishable, and ran across boggy land, where it was only too easy to plunge over one's boot-tops in oozy peat. Miss Moseley found the way like a pioneer; she had often been there before and remembered just what places were treacherous and just where it was possible to use a swinging bough for a help. By following in her footsteps the party got safely over without serious wettings, and sat down to take breath for a few minutes on some smooth, glacier-ground rocks that topped the ridge they had been scaling. They were now at some height above the valley, and the prospect was magnificent. For at least ten miles they could trace the windings of the river, and taller and more distant mountain peaks had come into view.

"Some people say that Craigwen Valley's very like the Rhine," volunteered Ulyth. "It hasn't any castles, of course, except at Llangarmon, but the scenery's just as lovely."

"Nice to think it's British then," rejoiced Merle. "Wales can hold its own in the way of mountains and lakes. People have no need to go abroad for them. What's New Zealand like, Rona?"

"We've ripping rivers there," replied the Cuckoo, "bigger than this by lots, and with tree-ferns up in the bush. This isn't bad, though, as far as it goes. What's that place over across on the opposite hill?"

"Where the light's shining? Oh, that's Llanfairgwyn! There's a village and a church. We've only been once. It's rather a long way, because you have to cross the ferry at Glanafon before you can get to the other side of the river."

Angela Brazil

"And what's that big white house in the trees, with the flag?"

"That's Plas Cafn. It's *the* place in the neighbourhood, you know," said Stephanie, fondly fingering her necklace.

"I don't know. How should I?"

"Well, you know it now, at any rate."

"Does it belong to toffs?"

"It belongs to Lord and Lady Glyncraig. They live there for part of the year."

"Oh!" said Rona. She put her chin on her hand and surveyed the distant mansion for several moments in silence. "I reckon they're stuck up," she remarked at last.

"I believe they're considered nice. I've never spoken to them," replied Ulyth.

"I have," put in Stephanie complacently. "I went to tea once at Plas Cafn. It was when Father was Member for Rotherford. Lord Glyncraig knew him in Parliament, of course, and he happened to meet Father and me just when we were walking past the gate at Plas Cafn, and asked us in to tea."

Merle, Addie, and Ulyth smiled. This visit, paid four years ago, was the standing triumph of Stephanie's life. She never forgot, nor allowed any of her schoolfellows to forget, that she had been entertained by the great people of the neighbourhood.

"He wasn't Lord Glyncraig then; he was only Sir John Mitchell, Baronet. He's been raised to a peerage since," said Merle, willing to qualify some of the glory of Stephanie's reminiscences.

"We don't grow peers in Waitoto, or baronets either, for the matter of that," observed Rona. "I don't guess they're wanted out with us. We'd have no place in the bush for a Lord Glyncraig."

"You'd better claim acquaintance with him, as your name's Mitchell too. How proud he'd be of the honour!" teased Addie.

Coral flooded the whole of the Cuckoo's face. She had begun to understand the difference between her rough upbringing and the refined homes of the other girls, and she resented the sneers that were often made at her expense.

"Our butcher at home is Joseph Mitchell," hinnied Merle.

"Mitchell's a common enough name," said Ulyth. "I know two families in Scotland and some people at Plymouth all called Mitchell. They're none of them related to each other, and probably not to Merle's butcher or to Lord Glyncraig."

"Nor to me," said Rona. "I'm a democrat, and I glory in it. Stephanie's welcome to her grand friends if she likes them."

"I do like them," sighed Stephanie plaintively. "I love aristocratic people and nice houses and things. Why shouldn't I? You needn't grin, Addie Knighton; you'd know them yourself if you could. When I come out I'd like to be presented at Court, and go to a ball where the people are all dukes and duchesses and earls and countesses. It would be worth while dancing with a duke, especially if he wore the Order of the Garter!"

"Until that glorious day comes you'll have to dance with poor little me for a partner," giggled Merle.

Angela Brazil

"Aren't you all rested? We shall get no blackberries if we don't hurry on," called Miss Moseley from the other end of the rock.

Everybody scrambled up immediately and set out again over the bracken-covered hill-side. Another half-mile and they had reached the bourne of their expedition. The narrow track through the gorse and fern widened suddenly into a lane, a lane with very high, unmortared walls, over which grew a variety of bramble with a particularly luscious fruit. Every connoisseur of blackberries knows what a difference there is between the little hard seedy ones that commonly flourish in the hedges and the big juicy ones with the larger leaves. Nature had been prodigal here, and a bounteous harvest hung within easy reach.

"They are as big as mulberries—and oh, such heaps and heaps!" exclaimed Addie ecstatically. "No, Merle, you wretch, this is my branch! Don't poach, you wretch! Go farther on, can't you!"

"I wish we could send the jam to the hospital when it's made," sighed Merle.

The party spread itself out; some of the girls climbed to the top of the wall, so that they could reach what grew on the sunnier side, and a few skirted round over a gate into a field, where a ruined cottage was also covered with brambles. They worked down the lane by slow degrees, picking hard as they went. At the end a sudden rushing roar struck upon the ear, and without even waiting for a signal from Miss Moseley the girls with one accord hopped over a fence, and ran up a slight incline. The voice of the waterfall was calling, and the impulse to obey was irresistible. At the top of the slope they stopped, for they had reached a natural platform that overlooked the gorge. The scene rivalled one of the beauty-spots of Switzerland. The Porth Powys stream, flowing between precipitous rocks, fell two hundred feet in a series of four splendid cascades. The rugged crags on either side were thickly covered with a forest of fir and larch, and here and there a taller stone-pine reared its darker head above the silvery green. Dashing, roaring, leaping, shouting, the water poured down in a never-ceasing volume: the white spray rose up in clouds, wetting the girls' faces; the sound was like an endless chorus of hallelujahs.

"Porth Powys is in fine form to-day. There must have been rain up in the mountains last night," remarked Ulyth. "What do you think of it, Rona?"

"It's a champion! I'm going to climb down there and get at the edge."

"No, you won't!" said Miss Moseley sharply. "Nobody is to go a single step nearer. You must all come back into the lane now, and get on with blackberry-picking. Your baskets are only half full yet."

Very reluctantly the girls followed. The fall exercised a fascination over them, and they could have stayed half an hour watching its white swirl. They did not wish, however, to earn the reputation of slackers. Two other parties had gone out blackberrying that afternoon, and there would be keen competition as to which would bring back the most pounds. They set to work again, therefore, with enthusiasm, counting stained fingers and scratches as glorious wounds earned in the good cause. Rona picked with zeal, but she had a preoccupied look on her face.

"Say, I liked that waterfall," she remarked to Ulyth. "One can't see anything of it down in this old lane. I'm going to get a better view."

Angela Brazil

"You mustn't go off on your own," commanded Ulyth. "Miss Moseley will report you if you do!"

"Don't excite yourself. I only said I was going to get a better view. It's quite easy."

Rona put her basket in a safe place, and with the aid of a hazel bush climbed to the top of the wall. Apparently the prospect did not satisfy her.

"I'm going a stave higher still. Keep your hair on!" she shouted down to Ulyth, and began swarming up the bole of a huge old oak-tree that abutted on the wall. She was strong and active as a boy, and had soon scrambled to where the branches forked. A mass of twisted ivy hung here, and raising herself with its aid, she stood on an outstretched bough.

"It's ripping! I can see a little bit of the fall; I'll see it better if I get over on to that other branch."

"Take care!" called Miss Moseley from below.

Rona started. She had not known the mistress was so near. The movement upset her decidedly unstable balance; she clutched hard at the ivy, but it gave way in her fingers; there was a sudden crash and a smothered shriek.

White as a ghost, Miss Moseley climbed the wall, expecting to find the prostrate form of her pupil on the other side. To her surprise she saw nothing of the sort. Near at hand, however, came a stifled groan.

"Rona, where are you?" shrieked the distracted governess.

"Here," spluttered the voice of the Cuckoo; "inside the tree.

The beastly old thing's rotten, and I've tumbled to the very bottom of the trunk!"

"Are you hurt?"

"No, nothing to speak of."

"Here's a pretty go!" murmured the girls, who all came running at the sound of shouts. "How's she going to get out again?"

"Can't you climb up?" urged Miss Moseley.

"No, I can't stir an inch; I'm wedged in somehow."

What was to be done? The affair waxed serious. Miss Moseley, with a really heroic effort, and much help from the girls, managed to scale the tree and look down into the hollow trunk. She could just see Rona's scared face peeping up at her many feet below.

"Can you put up your hand and let me pull you?"

"No; I tell you I'm wedged as tight as a sardine."

"We shall have to send for help then. May and Kathleen, run as quickly as you can down the lane. There's a farm at the bottom of the hill. Tell them what's the matter."

"I hope to goodness they'll understand English!" murmured Merle.

"Will I have to stop here always?" demanded a tragic voice within the tree. "Shall you be able to feed me, or will I have to starve? How long does it take to die of hunger?"

"You won't die just yet," returned Miss Moseley, laughing a little in spite of herself. "We'll get you out in course of time."

"I guess I'd better make my will, though. Has anybody got a pencil and paper, and will they please write it down and send it home? I want to leave my saddle to Pamela Higson, and Jake is to have the bridle and whip—I always liked him better than Billy, though I pretended I didn't. Jane Peters may have my writing-desk—much she writes, though!—and Amabel Holt my old doll. That's all I've left in New Zealand. Ulyth can take what I've got at school—'twon't be any great shakes to her, I expect. You didn't tell me how long it takes to die!"

"Cheer up! There's not the slightest danger," Miss Moseley continued to assure her.

"It's all very well to say 'cheer up' when you're standing safe on the top," said the gloomy voice of the imprisoned dryad. "It feels a different matter when you're boxed up tight with tree all round you. It's jolly uncomfortable. Where are the girls?"

"Here's one," replied Ulyth, climbing the tree to relieve poor Miss Moseley, who gladly retired in her favour. "I'm going to stay and talk to you till somebody comes to get you out. Oh, here are May and Kathleen at last! What a fearful time they've been!"

The two messengers came panting back with many excuses for their delay. It was a long way down the lane to the farm, and when they arrived there they had considerable difficulty in explaining their errand. No one could understand English except a little boy, who was only half-able to translate their remarks into Welsh. They had at length made the farmer realize what had happened, and he had promised to come at once. In the course of a few minutes they were followed by David Jones and his son, Idwal, bearing a rope, an axe, and a saw, and looking rather dismayed at the task in store for them. It proved indeed a matter of considerable difficulty to rescue Rona without hurting her; a portion of the tree-trunk was obliged to be sawn away before she could obtain sufficient room to help to free herself, and it was only after an hour's hard work that she stood at last in safety on the ground.

"How do you feel?" asked Miss Moseley anxiously, fearing broken bones or a sprain from the final effort of extraction.

"Well, I guess it's taken the bounce out of me. I'm as stiff as a rheumatic cat! Oh, I'll get back to school somehow, don't alarm yourself! I'm absolutely starving for tea. Good-bye, you wood-demon; you nearly finished me!" and Rona shook her fist at the offending oak-tree as a parting salute.

"She called it demon to rhyme with lemon!" gurgled Addie, almost sobbing with mirth as she followed, holding Merle's arm. "The Cuckoo will cause me to break a blood-vessel some day. It hurts me most dreadfully to laugh. I've got a stitch in my side. Oh dear! I wonder whatever she'll go and do next?"

Angela Brazil

CHAPTER V

ON SUFFERANCE

"Scratch, scratch, scratch,
Scratch went the old black hen!
Every fowl that scrapes in the barn
Can scratch as well as your pen!"

So sang Rona, bounding noisily one afternoon into No. 3, Room 5, and popping her hands from behind over Ulyth's eyes as the latter sat writing at a table near the window.

"What are you always scratching away for? Can't you finish your work at prep.? Why don't you come downstairs and play basket-ball? You're mighty studious all of a sudden. What have you got here?"

Ulyth flushed crimson with annoyance, and turned her sheets of foolscap hastily over to hide them from her room-mate's prying eyes.

"You're not to touch my papers, Rona! I've told you that before."

"Well, I wasn't touching them. Looking's not touching, anyway. What are you doing? It's queer taste to sit scribbling here half your spare time."

"What I was doing is my own concern, and no business of yours."

"Now you're riled," said the Cuckoo, sitting down easily on her bed. "I didn't mean any harm. I always seem sticking my foot into it somehow."

Ulyth sighed. Nobody in the school realized how much she had to put up with from her irrepressible room-mate, whose hearty voice, extraordinary expressions, and broad notions of fun grated upon her sensitive nature. Rona did not appreciate in the least the heroic sacrifice that Ulyth was making. It had never occurred to her that she might be placed in another dormitory, and that she only remained on sufferance in No. 3. She admired Ulyth immensely, and was quite prepared to take her as a model, but at present the copy was very far indeed from the original. The mistresses had instituted a vigorous crusade against Rona's loud voice and uncon-ventional English, and she was really making an effort to improve; but the habits of years are not effaced in a few weeks, and she still scandalized the authorities considerably. Ulyth could tolerate her when she kept to her own side of the bedroom, but to have meddlesome fingers interfering with her private possessions was the last straw to her burden of endurance.

"Do you understand?" she repeated emphatically. "You're not to touch my papers at all!"

"All serene! I won't lay a finger on them—honest—sure!" returned the Cuckoo, chanting her words to the air of "Swanee River", and drumming an accompaniment on the bedpost. "What d'you think Stephanie called me just now? She said I was an unlicked cub."

"Oh, surely she didn't! Are you certain?"

"Heard her myself. She said it to my face and tittered. You bet I'll pay her out somehow. Miss Stephanie Radford needs taking down a peg. Oh, don't alarm yourself, I'll do it neatly! There'll be no clumsy bungling about it. Well, if you won't go down and play basket-ball I shall. It's more fun than sitting up here."

As the door banged behind Rona, Ulyth heaved an ecstatic "Thank goodness!" She sat for a few moments trying to regain her composure before she recommenced the writing at which she had been interrupted. The manuscript on which she was engaged was very precious. She had set herself no less a task than to write a book. The subject had come to her suddenly one morning as she lay awake in bed, and she regarded it as an inspiration. She would make a story about The Woodlands, and bring in all the girls she knew. It was no use struggling with a historical plot or a romance of the war—she had tried these, and stuck fast in the first chapters; it was better to employ the material close at hand, and weave her tale from the every-day incidents which happened in the school. So she had begun, and though she floundered a little at the difficulty of transferring her impressions to paper, she was making distinct progress.

"I'd never dare to have it published, of course," she ruminated. "Still, it's a beginning, and I shall like to read it over to myself. I think there are some rather neat bits in it, especially that shot at Addie and Stephie. How wild they'd be if they knew! But there's no fear of that. I'll take good care nobody finds out."

When to make time to go on with her literary composition was the difficulty. It was hard to snatch even an occasional half-hour during the day. Where there is a will, however, there is generally also a way, and Ulyth hit upon the plan of getting up very early in the morning and writing while Rona was still asleep. The Cuckoo never stirred until the seven o'clock bell rang, when she would awake noisily, with many yawns and stretchings of arms, so Ulyth flattered herself that her secret was absolutely safe.

Where to hide the precious papers was another problem. She did not dare to put them in any of her drawers, her desk would not lock, and her little jewel-box was too small to contain them.

The fireplace in the bedroom had an old-fashioned chimney-piece that was fitted with a loose wooden mantel-board, from which hung a border of needlework. It was quite easy to lift up this board and slip the papers between it and the chimney-piece; the border completely screened the hiding-place, and, except at a spring-cleaning, the arrangement was not likely to be disturbed. Ulyth congratulated herself greatly upon her ingenuity. It was interesting to have a secret which nobody even guessed. She often looked at the chimney-piece, and chuckled as she thought of what lay concealed there.

The days were rapidly closing in now, and the time between tea and preparation, which only a few weeks ago was devoted to a last game of tennis or a run by the stream, was perforce spent by the schoolroom fire. It was only a short interval, not long enough to make any elaborate occupation worth while, so the girls sat knitting in the twilight and chatting until the bell rang for evening work.

One afternoon, when tea was finished, Ulyth, instead of joining the others as usual, walked upstairs to put away some specimens in the Museum. She passed V B classroom as she did so, and heard smothered peals of mirth issuing from behind the half-closed door.

"What are they doing?" she thought. "I believe I'll go and see." But catching Rona's laugh above the rest, she changed her mind, walked on, and bestowed her fossils carefully in a spare corner of one of the cases. Meanwhile, the group assembled round the fire in V B were enjoying themselves. The room was growing dusk, but, seated on the hearthrug, Addie Knighton could see quite sufficiently to read aloud extracts from a document she was perusing, extracts to which the others listened with thrilling interest, interspersed with comments.

"'The girls of the Oaklands'," so she read, "'were a rather peculiar and miscellaneous set, especially those in the Lower Fifth. Scarcely any of them could be called pretty—'" ("Oh! oh!" howled the attentive circle.) "'One of them, Valerie Chadford, imagined herself so, and gave herself fearful airs in consequence; she was very set up at knowing smart people, and often bragged about it.'" ("I'll never forgive her, never!" screamed Stephanie.) "'The twins, Pearl and Doris, were fat, stodgy girls, who wore five-and-a-halfs in shoes and had twenty-seven-inch waists.'" ("Oh! Won't Merle and Alice be just frantic when they hear?") "'But even they were more interesting than Nellie Clacton, who usually sat with her mouth open, as if she was trying to catch flies.'" ("Does she mean me?" gasped Mary Acton indignantly.) "'Florence Tulliver was inclined to be snarly, and often said mean things about other people behind their backs.'" ("I'll say something now!" declared Gertrude Oliver.) "'And Annie Ryton was—'" but here Addie broke off abruptly and exploded.

"Go on! Go on!" commanded the girls.

"It's too lovely!" spluttered Addie. "O—ho—ho! So that's what she thinks of me, is it?"

"Read it, can't you?"

"Here, give the paper to me!"

"No, no! I'll go on—but—I didn't know my eyes were like faded gooseberries, and my hair like dried seaweed!"

"Has she described herself!" asked Stephanie.

"I haven't come to it yet. Oh yes! here we are, farther on: 'Our heroine, Morvyth Langton, was an unusually—'"

But here Addie stopped abruptly, for a blazing little fury stood in the doorway.

"Addie Knighton, how dare you? How dare you? Give me that paper this instant!"

"No, no! It's much too interesting. Let go! Don't be silly! How can you? Oh, what a shame!" as Ulyth in her anger tore the manuscript across and flung it into the fire.

"Whew! Now you've gone and done it!" whistled Rona.

Ulyth was holding down the last flaming fragment with the poker. When it had expired she turned to the guilty circle. "Who took my papers from my bedroom?"

Her voice was sharp, and her eyes fixed full on Rona.

"I didn't touch them. I never laid so much as a finger on them," protested the Cuckoo.

"But you told someone where they were?"

Rona winked in reply. Yes, alas! winked consciously and deliberately. (It was well for her that Miss Moseley was not in the room.)

"I knew you'd got something there," she admitted. "Were you such an innocent as to think I never saw you scribbling away hard in the early mornings? Why, I was foxing! I used to watch you while I was snoring, and nearly died with laughing because you never found me out."

If eyes could slay, Ulyth's would have finished Rona at that moment. But Addie Knighton, whose suspension of mirth had been merely a species of temporary paralysis, now relapsed into a choking series of guffaws, in which the others joined boisterously.

"I can't—get—over—seaweed—and faded gooseberries!" crowed Addie hysterically.

"I don't catch flies with my open mouth!" shouted Mary Acton, suspending her knitting in her indignation.

"Will somebody please measure the twins' waists?" bleated Christine.

"I didn't say it was meant for any of you. If the cap fits, put it on. Listeners hear no good of themselves, and no more do people who read what isn't intended for them. It serves you all right, so there!" and Ulyth flounced out of the room.

She ran straight up to her bedroom, and burst into tears. It was such a tragi-comedy ending to her literary ambition. She would rather the girls had been more indignant than that they had laughed so much.

"I'll never write another line again," she resolved; and then she thought of the binding she had always intended to have on her first published book, and wept harder.

"Ulyth," said the Cuckoo, stealing in rather shamefacedly,

"I'm really frightfully sorry if you're riled. I didn't know you cared all that much about those old papers. I told Addie, as a joke, and she went and poked them out. I think they were fine. It was a shame to burn them. Can't you write them over again?"

"Never!" Ulyth replied, wiping her eyes. "Rona, you don't realize what damage you've done. There! oh yes, I'll forgive you, but if you want to keep friends with me, don't go and do anything of the sort again, that's all!"

Ulyth felt a little shy of meeting her class-mates after their discovery of the very unflattering description she had written of them, but the girls were good-natured and did not bear malice. They treated the whole affair as an intense joke, and even took to calling one another by the assumed names of the story. They composed extra portions, including a lurid description of Ulyth herself, illustrated by rapid sketches on the black-board. The disappointed authoress took it with what calm she could muster. She knew they meant to tease, and the fewer sparks they could raise from her the sooner they would desist and let the matter drop. It would probably serve as a target for Addie's wit till the end of the term, unless the excitement of the newly formed ambulance class chased it from her memory. The Woodlanders were trying to do their duty by their country, and all the girls were enthusiastically practising bandaging.

"I wish we'd some real patients to bind up," sighed Merle one day, as V B took its turn under Nurse Griffith's instructions.

"I'd be sorry for them if they were left to your tender mercies," retorted Mavis, who had been posing as patient. "My arm's sore yet with your vigorous measures."

"What nonsense! I was as gentle as a lamb."

"A curious variety of lamb then, with a wolf inside."

"I believe The Woodlands would make a gorgeous hospital," suggested Addie hopefully. "When we're through our course we might have some real patients down and nurse them."

"Don't you think it! The Rainbow won't carry ambulance lessons as far as that!"

CHAPTER VI

QUITS

Ulyth, brushing her hair before the looking-glass one morning, hummed cheerily.

"You seem in spirits," commented Rona, from the washstand. "It's more than I am. Miss Lodge was a pig yesterday. She said my dictation was a disgrace to the school, and I'd got to stop in during the interval this morning and write out all the wrong words a dozen times each. It's too sickening! I'd no luck yesterday. Phyllis Chantrey had my book to correct, and her writing and mine are such opposite poles, we daren't try it on."

"Try what on?" asked Ulyth, pausing with the brush in her hand.

"Why, the exchange dodge, you know."

"I don't know."

"Don't you take dictation in V B? Well, in our form we get it twice a week, and Miss Lodge makes us correct each other's books. We make it up to try and exchange with a girl whose writing's pretty like one's own; then, you see, we can alter things neatly, and allow full marks. It generally works, but it didn't yesterday."

Ulyth's face was a study.

"You mean to tell me you correct each other's mistakes!"

"Why not?" said Rona, not the least abashed. "Miss Lodge never finds out."

Ulyth collapsed into a chair. What was she to do with such a girl?

"Don't you know it's the most atrocious cheating?"

"Is it? Why, the whole form does it," returned the Cuckoo unconcernedly.

"Then they're abominable little wretches, and don't deserve to be candidates for the Camp-fire League. I'm thoroughly ashamed of them. Have they no sense of honour?"

The Cuckoo was looking perplexed.

"Ulyth Stanton, you're always rounding something new on me," she sighed. "I can't keep up with you. I keep my hair tidy now, and don't leave my things lying round the room, and I try to give a sort of twitter instead of laughing, and I've dropped ever so many words you object to, and practise walking down the passage with a book on my head. What more do you want?"

"A great deal," said Ulyth gravely. "Didn't you learn honour at home?"

"Catch Mrs. Barker!"

"But surely your father—?"

"I saw so little of Dad. He was out all day, and sometimes off for weeks together at our other block. When he was at home he didn't care to be bothered overmuch."

An amazed pity was taking the place of Ulyth's indignation. This was, indeed, fallow ground. Mrs. Arnold's comment flashed across her mind:

"What an opportunity for a Torch-bearer!"

"I don't want to be turned into a prig," urged the Cuckoo.

"You needn't. There's a certain amount of slang and fun that's allowable, but *noblesse oblige* must always come first. You don't understand French yet? Well, never mind. All that matters is that you simply must realize, Rona—do listen, please—that all of us here, including you, mustn't—couldn't —cheat at lessons. For your own sake, and for the sake of the school, you must stop it."

"You think a lot of the school!"

"And quite right too! The school stands to us for what the State does to grown-up people. We've got to do our best to keep the tone up. Cheating brings it down with a run. It's as bad as tearing up treaties."

"Go ahead. Rub it in," returned the Cuckoo, beginning to whistle a trifle defiantly.

She thought the matter over, nevertheless, and returned to the subject that night when they were going to bed.

"Ulyth, I told the girls exactly what you said about them. My gracious, you should have seen their faces! Boiled lobsters weren't in it. That hit about the Camp-fire Guild seemed specially to floor them. I don't fancy, somehow, there'll be any more correcting done in dictation. You've touched them up no end."

"I'm extremely glad if what I said has brought them to their senses," declared Ulyth.

Rona got on tolerably well among her comrades, but there was one exception. With Stephanie she was generally in a state of guerrilla warfare. The latter declared that the vulgar addition to the school was an outrage on the feelings of those who had been better brought up. Stephanie had ambitions towards society with a big S, and worshipped titles. She would have liked the daughter of a duke for a schoolfellow, but so far no member of the aristocracy had condescended to come and be educated at The Woodlands. Stephanie felt injured that Miss Bowes and Miss Teddington should have accepted such a girl as Rona, and lost no opportunity of showing that she thought the New Zealander very far below the accepted standard. The Cuckoo's undoubted good looks were perhaps another point in her disfavour. The school beauty did not easily yield place to a rival, and though she professed to consider Rona's complexion too high-coloured, she had a sneaking consciousness that it was superior to her own.

During the summer holidays Stephanie had taken part in a pageant that was held in aid of a charity near her home. As Queen of the Roses she had occupied a rather important position, and her portrait, in her beautiful fancy costume, had appeared in several of the leading ladies' newspapers. Stephanie's features were good, and the photograph had been a very happy one—"glorified out of all knowledge" said some of the girls; so the photographer had exhibited it in his window, and altogether more notice had been taken of it than was perhaps salutary for the original. Stephanie had brought a copy back to school, and it now adorned her bedroom mantelpiece. She was never tired of descanting upon the pageant, and telling about all the aristocratic people who had come to see it. According to her account the very flower of the neighbourhood had been present, and had taken special notice of her. A girl who had so lately consorted with the county could not be expected to tolerate a tyro from the backwoods. Stephanie was too well brought up to allow herself to be often openly rude; her taunts were generally ingeniously veiled, but they were none the less aggravating for that. The Cuckoo might be callow in some respects, but in others she was very much up-to-date. Though she would look obtuse, and pretend not to understand, as a matter of fact not a gibe was lost upon her, and she kept an exact account of the score.

One morning, early in December, Miss Teddington, who was distributing the contents of the postbag, handed Stephanie a small parcel. It was only a few days after the latter's birthday, and, supposing it to be a belated present, the mistress did not ask the usual questions by which she regulated her pupils' correspondence. The letters were always given out immediately after breakfast, and the girls took them upstairs to read in their dormitories during the quarter of an hour in which they made their beds and tidied their rooms. This morning, just as Ulyth was shaking her pillow, Rona came in, chuckling to herself. The Cuckoo's eyes twinkled like stars.

"D'you want some sport?" she asked. "If you do, come with me, and have the time of your life!"

Ulyth put down the pillow, and hesitated. Fifteen minutes was not too long an allowance for all she was expected to do in her room. But Rona's manner was inviting. She wanted to see what the fun was. The temptress held the door open, and beckoned beguilingly.

"All serene!" yielded Ulyth.

Rona seized her by the arm and dragged her delightedly down the passage.

"Now you're chummy," she murmured. "Whatever you do, though, don't make a noise and give the show away!"

Still in the dark as to the Cuckoo's intentions, Ulyth allowed herself to be led to Dormitory 2, No. 4, at the opposite side of the house. We have mentioned before that the bedrooms at The Woodlands were very spacious—so large, indeed, that each was partitioned into four cubicles divided by lath-and-plaster walls. A passage inside the dormitory gave access to the cubicles, which were in fact separate little bedrooms, except that the partition walls, for purposes of ventilation, did not reach the ceiling. At present the fourth cubicle in Dormitory 2 was unoccupied, but its furniture was rather curiously arranged. One of the beds had been pulled close against the partition, and a chest of drawers, with the drawers removed, had been placed upon it.

"I fixed it up last night, and it was a job," whispered the Cuckoo. "Good thing I'm strong. Now we've got to climb on that, and you'll see what you'll see!"

Ulyth had an uneasy consciousness that she ought not to be mixed up in such a business; but, after all, the girls often scrambled up and peeped into one another's cubicles for a joke, so her action would not be without precedent. She was a very human person, and liked fun as well as anybody. With extreme caution she and Rona mounted the chest of drawers, trying not to make the slightest noise. Their eyes were just on a level with the top of the partition, and they had a good view of the next cubicle. The occupants, Stephanie and her room-mate, Beth Broadway, were far too absorbed to think of looking up towards the ceiling. Their attention was concentrated on the parcel which had arrived by the post. It contained a small bottle, carefully packed in shavings, and also a typewritten letter, the purport of which seemed to electrify Stephanie.

"It's the most extraordinary thing I've ever heard!" she was saying. "Beth, just listen to this."

And she read aloud:

"66 HOLBORN VIADUCT,
LONDON.

"DEAR MADAM,

"Having seen your portrait, as a noted beauty, published in *The Princess*, *The Ladies' Court Journal*, and other leading pictorials, we venture to submit to you a sample of our famous Eau de Venus, an invaluable adjunct to the toilet of any lady possessing a delicate complexion. It is a perfectly harmless, fragrantly scented fluid, which, if applied daily after breakfast, produces a rose-leaf bloom which is absolutely incomparable. As it is a new preparation, we are anxious to submit it to a few ladies of influence in the fashionable world, feeling sure that, once used, they will recommend it.

"We shall esteem it a great favour if you will graciously try the enclosed sample. We do not ask for testimonials, but any expression of appreciation from one who figured so admirably as Queen of the Roses at the Barrfield Pageant would be to us a source of immense gratification.

"May we recommend that the preparation be applied immediately after breakfast, as its ingredients are more potent to the delicate pores of the skin if used at that period of the morning.

"With apologies for troubling you, and hoping you will condescend to give our Eau de Venus at least a trial,

"We remain,

"Faithfully yours,

"RENAN, MARIETTE, ET CIE,
Parfumeurs."

"How very peculiar!" gasped Beth, much impressed.

"It must be because they saw my photo in the papers," said Stephanie. She was trying to speak casually, and not to appear too flattered, but her eyes shone. "I believe that pageant made rather a sensation, and of course, well, I was the principal figure in it. I suppose I shall have to try this Eau de Venus."

"It's in a funny little bottle," commented Beth.

"Samples generally are. They never send you very much of a thing. They want you to buy a big bottle afterwards."

Stephanie carefully removed the cork. The preparation seemed to be of a pink, milky description.

"It smells of violets," she said, offering the bottle for Beth to sniff.

"I should certainly try it, if I were you," recommended

the latter.

"It says it's quite harmless," continued Stephanie, referring to the letter, "and should be used immediately after breakfast. Well, there's no time like the present!"

If there was a curious agitation on the other side of the partition, neither girl noticed it. Stephanie poured some of the liquid into her hand and rubbed it over her face. Then she turned to the looking-glass.

"It seems very pink and queer! It's all in red streaks!"

"Perhaps you've put on too much. Wipe some of it off," advised Beth.

Vigorous measures with a sponge followed, and Stephanie anxiously surveyed the result.

"It won't come off!" she faltered. "Oh, what have I done to myself? I'm all red smears!"

Her dismay was too much for one at least on the other side of the partition. Rona broke into a loud, cackling laugh. One swift glance upwards and Stephanie realized that she was the victim of a practical joke. It took her exactly three seconds to reach the next cubicle.

"So it's you, is it?" she exploded. "Well, Ulyth Stanton, I am astonished! Evil communications corrupt good manners, and yours smack of the backwoods."

"Don't throw it on Ulyth; she knew nothing about it," retorted the chuckling Cuckoo belligerently. "It's my business, and I don't mind telling you so!"

Angela Brazil

"I might have known, you—you utter cad! You don't deserve to be in a school among ladies!"

"Go on. Pitch it as strong as you like. The cub's quits with you now for all your airs and your nastiness."

"Oh, don't!" protested Ulyth, interfering in much distress. "Rona, do stop! I'd no idea you meant to play such a dreadful trick on Stephie."

"You must have known something of it, or you wouldn't have come to look on. I expect you were at the bottom of it," sneered Stephanie; "so don't try to sneak out of it, Ulyth Stanton. Your precious joke has marked me for life."

"No, no! It's only cochineal and milk. I got it from the cook," put in the Cuckoo.

"It's stained her face all over, though," said Beth Broadway reproachfully.

"I shall go straight to Miss Bowes," whimpered Stephanie.

"I wouldn't do that if I were you," said Ulyth. "Try some methylated spirit first. I'll give you some from my room."

The remedy proved efficacious. The stains yielded to gentle rubbing, and the four girls flew in a wild hurry to make their beds, three much relieved and one naughtily exultant.

"I've paid out Stephie," panted Rona, tucking in her blankets anyhow. "I felt proud of that letter. Made it up with the help of advertisements in the *Illustrated Journal*. Then I typed it in the study while Teddie was out. You didn't know I could type? Learnt how on the voyage, from a girl who'd a typewriter on board with her. I laid on the butter pretty thick.

I knew Steph would swallow it to any amount. Oh, didn't she just look flattered? It was prime! The under-housemaid posted the parcel for me."

"Stephie'll never forgive you!"

"Much I care!"

CHAPTER VII

THE CUCKOO'S PROGRESS

"Your bear cub still needs taming, Ulyth," said Gertrude Oliver. "She spilt her coffee this morning—such a mess on the tablecloth! I wish I didn't sit next to her. I felt like Alice at the March Hare's tea-party."

"It was half Maud's fault; she jerked her elbow," pleaded Ulyth in extenuation.

"Oh, you can't whitewash her, so don't try! I won't say she isn't better than when she arrived, but there's room for improvement."

"She's much slimmer. I suppose it must have been the voyage that had made her grow so fat in September."

"I wish, at any rate, you could get her out of using those dreadful backwoods expressions. It's high time she dropped them. She's been here nearly a full term."

Ulyth thought so too, and the next time she found a suitable opportunity she tackled Rona on the subject.

"You're too nice to speak in such a queer way. You've no

idea how it spoils you," she urged. "You could be another girl if you'd only take a little trouble."

"What's the use? Who minds what I'm like?" returned the Cuckoo a trifle defiantly.

"I do," said Ulyth emphatically.

"Not really?"

"Indeed I do. I care very much. You came over here to be my friend, and there are many things I want in a friend."

"I didn't know you cared," replied Rona in a softened voice. "No one ever did before—except Dad, when he said I was a savage."

"Don't you want to show him what you can grow into?" asked Ulyth eagerly. "Think how surprised and pleased he'll be when he sees you again!"

"There's something in that."

"There's a great deal in it. I know I often make myself do things I don't want because of Mother; she's such a darling, and—" She stopped short, realizing too late the mistake she was making.

"I can't remember Mother," answered Rona, turning away with a suggestive cough. "It's all very well for you."

Ulyth could have bitten her tongue out. She said no more, for she knew her room-mate well enough by this time to have learnt that sympathy must be offered with the utmost discretion. The poor Cuckoo was only too well aware of the deficiencies in her home and upbringing, but the least hint of them from others immediately put her on the defensive. In her own way she was very proud, and though there was a vast difference between Stephanie's stinging remarks and Ulyth's well-meant kindness, anything that savoured of compassion wounded her dignity.

The conversation brought urgently to Ulyth a question which had been disturbing her, and which she had persistently tried to banish from her thoughts. Where was Rona going to spend Christmas? So far as anyone knew she had not a friend or relation in the British Isles. Miss Bowes and Miss Teddington always went away for the holidays, and The Woodlands was left in the charge of servants. Rona could not stay at the school, surely? Had Miss Bowes made any arrangement for her? Ulyth vacillated for at least five minutes, then took out her writing-case and began a letter home.

"BEST-BELOVED MOTHERKINS,

"I am such a nasty, horrid, selfish thing! In every one of your letters you have hinted and hinted and hinted that we should ask Rona for Christmas. You wouldn't say it outright until you were sure I wanted it. That was just the rub. I didn't want it. I'm afraid even now I don't quite. I've had her all the term, and I thought it would be so blissful to be without her for four whole weeks, and have you and Father and Oswald and Dorothy and Peter just to myself. But oh, Motherkins, she's such a lonely waif of a girl! I'm so dreadfully sorry for her. She seems always out of everything. I'm sure she's never had a decent Christmas in her life. I believe she's fond of her father, though I don't think he took very much notice of her—she let out once that he was so disappointed she wasn't a boy. But Mrs. Barker, the housekeeper, must have been a most terrible person. Rona had no chance at all.

"Motherkins, she's never seen a real English home, and I'd

like to show her ours. Yes, I would, although in a way she'll spoil everything. May she sleep in the spare room, and let me have my own to myself? I could stand it then.

"Dearest darling, I really mean it; so will you write straight off to Miss Bowes before I have time to turn thoroughly horrid again?

"Your very loving daughter,

"ULYTH."

Having sent off the letter, and thus burnt her boats, Ulyth accepted the situation with what equanimity she could muster. Mrs. Stanton's invitation arrived by return of post, and was accepted with great relief by Miss Bowes, who had been wondering how to dispose of her pupil during the holidays. The Cuckoo received the news with such pathetic glee that Ulyth's heart smote her for not feeling more joyful herself.

"Are you sure you want me?" asked Rona wistfully.

"Of course we do, or we wouldn't ask you," replied Ulyth, hoping her fib might be forgiven.

"I'll try and not disgrace you," volunteered the Cuckoo.

A few days before the end of the term Rona received a letter from New Zealand. She rushed to Ulyth, waving it triumphantly.

"Dad's sent me this," she announced, showing a very handsome cheque. "I wrote to him three days after I got here, and told him my clothes looked rubbishy beside the other girls', and he tells me to rig myself out afresh. I suppose he

Angela Brazil

forgot about it till now. How'm I going to get the things? There isn't time to ask Miss Bowes to send for them before the holidays. Can I buy them at the place where you live?"

"Very well indeed, and Mother will help you to choose. I know she'll get you lovely clothes; she has such exquisite taste! She'll just enjoy it."

"And shan't I just? I'll give away every rag I brought with me from New Zealand. They'll come in for that rummage sale Teddie was telling us about."

The last lesson was finished, the last exercise written, even the last breakfast had been disposed of. The boxes, packed with great excitement the day before, were already dispatched, and four railway omnibuses were waiting to take the girls to Llangarmon Junction Station. Much to their regret, Miss Bowes would not allow them to go by Glanafon—the picturesque route by the ferry was reserved for summer weather. In winter, if the day happened to be stormy and the tide full, there was often great difficulty in crossing, the landing-place was muddy and slippery, and even if the train was not missed altogether (as sometimes happened) the small voyage was quite in the nature of an adventure.

Miss Bowes' wisdom was thoroughly justified on this particular morning, for there was a strong west wind, and the rain was pouring in torrents.

"It would have been lovely fun in the flat. There must be big waves on the river," declared Merle Denham, half aggrieved at missing such an interesting opportunity.

"Why, but look at the rain! You couldn't hold up an umbrella for half a second. It would be blown inside out directly.

You'd be as drenched as a drowned rat before you reached the train," preached her more prudent sister.

"And suppose you were blown off the stepping-stones into the river!" added Beth Broadway. "It would be a nice way of beginning the holidays! No. On a morning like this I'd rather have the omnibus. We shall at least start dry."

"I'm so glad you're taking Rona home with you," whispered Lizzie Lonsdale to Ulyth. "I should have asked her myself if you hadn't. It would have been a wretched Christmas for her to be left at school. I never saw anyone so pleased!"

The Cuckoo was indeed looking radiant at the golden prospect in store for her. Much to her surprise, everybody had been particularly nice to her that morning. Several girls had given her their addresses and asked her to write to them, Miss Bowes had been kindness itself, and even Miss Teddington, whose conduct was generally of a Spartan order, when bidding her good-bye in the study, had actually bestowed an abrupt peck of a kiss, a mark of favour never before known in the annals of the school. To be sure, she had followed it with a warning against relapsing into loud laughter in other people's houses; but then she was Miss Teddington!

Ulyth lived in Staffordshire, and the journey from North Wales was tedious; but what schoolgirl minds a long journey? To Rona all was new and delightful, and to Ulyth every telegraph-post meant that she was so much nearer home. The travellers had a royal reception, and kind, tactful Mrs. Stanton managed at once to put her young guest at ease, and make her feel that she was a welcome addition to the family circle. Oswald, Ulyth's elder brother, had come from Harrow only an hour before, and Dorothy and Peter, the two younger children, were prancing about in utmost enthusiasm at the exciting arrivals.

"Father hasn't come in yet?" asked Ulyth, when she had finished hugging her mother. "Well, it will be all the bigger treat when he does. Oh, Oswald, I didn't think you could grow so much in a term! Dorothy, darling, don't quite choke me! Peterkin, come and shake hands with Rona. Toby, do stop barking for half a moment! Where's Tabbyskins? And, please, show me the new parrot. Oh, isn't it lovely to be at home again!"

Almost the whole of the next day was spent by Mrs. Stanton, Ulyth, and their delighted visitor in a tour round various outfitting establishments—an exhilarating time for Rona, who was making her first acquaintance with the glories of English shops. Their purchases were highly satisfactory, and as Ulyth helped her friend to dress for dinner on Christmas Day she reviewed the result with the utmost complacency.

"Didn't I tell you Mother has good taste? Rona, you're lovely! This pale-blue dress suits you to a T. And the bronze slippers are so dainty; and your hair is so pretty. You can't think how it has improved lately."

"Do I look like other girls?" asked Rona, fingering the enamelled locket that had been given her that morning by Mr. and Mrs. Stanton.

"Rather! A great deal nicer than most. I'm proud of you. I wish they could all see you at The Woodlands."

"I'm glad if I shan't disgrace you. What a good thing Dad's cheque came just in time!"

In her new plumage the Cuckoo appeared turned into a tropical humming-bird. Ulyth had thought her good-looking before, but she had not realized that her room-mate was a beauty. She stared almost fascinated at the vision of blue eyes, coral cheeks, white neck, and ruddy-brown hair. Was this indeed the same girl who had arrived at school last September? It was like a transformation scene in the pantomime. Clothes undoubtedly exercise a great effect on some people, and Rona seemed to put away her backwoods manners with her up-country dresses. There was a dignity about her now and a desire to please which she had never shown at The Woodlands. She held herself straight, walked gracefully instead of shambling, and was careful to allow no uncouth expressions to escape her. Her behaviour was very quiet, as if she were watching others, or taking mental stock of how to comport herself. If occasionally she made some slight mistake she flushed crimson, but she never repeated it. She was learning the whole time, and the least gentle hint from Mrs. Stanton was sufficient for her. Miss Teddington need not have been afraid that the loud laugh would offend the ears of her friends; it never rang out once, and the high-pitched voice was subdued to wonderfully softened tones. For her hostess Rona evinced a species of worship. She would follow her about the house, content simply to be near her, and her face would light up at the slightest word addressed to her.

"The poor child just wanted a good mothering," said Mrs. Stanton to Ulyth. "It is marvellous how fast she is improving. You'll make something of your little wild bird after all. She's worth the trouble."

"I'd no idea she could grow into this," replied Ulyth. "Oh, Motherkins, you should have seen her at first! She was a very rough diamond."

"Aren't you glad to have a hand in the polishing? It will be such a triumph."

Two members of the household, at any rate, saw no fault in the visitor. Dorothy and Peter haunted her like small persistent ghosts, begging for stories about New Zealand. The accounts of her life in the bush were like a romance to them, and so fired their enthusiasm that in the intervals of playing soldiers they tried to emulate her adventures, and were found with a clothes-line in the garden making a wild attempt to lasso the much-enduring Toby.

"Rona's very good-natured with them," said Ulyth. "She doesn't mind how they pull her about, and Peter's most exhausting sometimes. I shouldn't like to carry him round the house on my back. Dorothy's perfectly insatiable for stories; it's always 'Tell us another!' How funny Oswald is at present. He's grown so outrageously polite all of a sudden. I suppose it's because he's in the Sixth now. He was very different last holidays. He's getting quite a 'lady's man'."

"The young folks are growing up very fast," commented Mr. Stanton in private. "It seems only yesterday that Oswald and Ulyth were babies. In another year or two we shall begin to think of twenty-first-birthday dances."

"Oh, don't talk of anything so dreadful!" said Mrs. Stanton in consternation. "They're my babies still. The party on Thursday is to be quite a children's affair."

Though "Motherkins" might regard the coming festivity as entirely of a juvenile character, the young people took it seriously. They practised dancing on the polished linoleum of the nursery every evening. Rona had had her first lessons at The Woodlands, and was making heroic efforts to remember what she had learnt.

"You'll get on all right," Ulyth encouraged her. "That last was ever so much better; you're dropping into it quite nicely.

You dance lightly, at any rate. Now try again with Oswald while I play. Ossie, I'm proud of you! Last Christmas you were a perfect duffer at it. Don't you remember how you sat out at the Warings'? You've improved immensely. Now go on!" and Ulyth began to play, with her eyes alternately on the piano and on the partners.

"I suppose a fellow has to get used to 'the light fantastic' sometime," remarked Oswald, as, after a successful five minutes' practice, he and Rona sat down to rest.

"Perhaps you'll have to dance with princesses at foreign Courts when you're a successful ambassador," laughed Ulyth.

"Is that what Oswald's going to be?" asked Rona.

"I'd have tried the Army or the Navy, but my wretched eyes cut me off from both; so it's no use, worse luck!" said Oswald. "I should like to get into the Diplomatic Service immensely though, if I could."

"Why can't you? I should think you could do anything you really wanted."

"Thanks for the compliment. But it's not so easy as it sounds. I wish I had a friend at Court."

"We don't know anybody in the Government," sighed Ulyth. "Not a solitary, single person. I've never even seen a member of Parliament, except, of course, Lord Glyncraig sometimes at church; but then I've never spoken to him. Stephanie had tea with him once. She doesn't let us forget that."

"I wish you'd had tea with him, and happened to mention particularly the extreme fascinations and abilities of your elder brother," laughed Oswald.

"Could Lord Glyncraig be of any use to you?" asked Rona. She had grown suddenly thoughtful.

"He could give me a nomination for the Diplomatic Service, and that would be just the leg-up I want. But it's no use joking; I'm not likely to get an introduction to him. I expect I shall have to go into business after all."

"I think when I was ten I must have been the most objectionable little imp on the face of creation," said Rona slowly. "I am ashamed of myself now."

"Why this access of penitence for bygone crimes?"

"Oh, nothing!" replied the Cuckoo, flushing. "I was only just thinking of something. Shall we try that new step again? I'm rested now."

"Yours to command, madam!" returned Oswald, with a mock bow.

*   *   *   *   *

Rona's visit to the Stantons was a delightful series of new impressions. She made her first acquaintance with the pantomime, and was alternately amused and thrilled as the story of "The Forty Thieves" unfolded itself upon the stage. Not even Peter watched with more round-eyed enthusiasm, and Mr. Stanton declared it was worth taking her for the mere pleasure of seeing her face when Ali Baba disappeared down a trap-door. As everything in England was fresh to her, she was a most easy guest to entertain, and she enjoyed every separate experience—from a visit to the public library with Mr. Stanton to toffee-making in the nursery with Peter and Dorothy.

Although it was a quiet Christmas in some respects, friends were hospitable, and included her in the various little invitations which were sent to Ulyth and Oswald; so her pretty dresses had a chance of being aired. The great event to the young folk was the party which was to be given at the Stantons' own house, and which was to be a kind of finish to the holidays. The girls revelled in every detail of preparation. They watched the carpet being taken up in the drawing-room, the large articles of furniture removed, and the door taken off its hinges. They sprinkled ball-room chalk on the boards of the floor, and slid indefatigably until the polish satisfied Ulyth's critical taste. They decorated the walls with flags and evergreens. They even offered their services in the kitchen, but met with so cool a reception from the busy cook that they did not venture to repeat the experiment, and consoled themselves with helping to write the supper menus instead.

"I think I've seen to everything," said Mrs. Stanton distractedly. "The flowers, and the fairy lamps, and the programmes, and those extra boxes of crackers, and the chocolates, and the ring for the trifle. You've seen about the music, Gerald?"

"Violin and piano," replied Mr. Stanton. "I'm feeling a thorough-going martyr. Giving even a simple children's hop means sitting in rooms without doors and living on turkey drumsticks for a fortnight afterwards!"

"Oh, we'll get the house straight again sooner than that! And you needn't eat grilled turkey unless you like."

"I don't appreciate parties."

"We must amuse the young folks, and it isn't a grand affair. If the children meet together they may as well dance as play games."

"Daddikins, how nasty you are!" exclaimed Ulyth, pursuing him to administer chastisement in the shape of smacking kisses. "You know you're looking forward to it quite as much as we are."

"That I deny *in toto*," groaned her father as he escaped to his snuggery, only to find it arranged as a dressing-room.

Ulyth wore white for the great occasion, with her best Venetian beads; and Rona had a palest sea-green gauzy voile, with fine stockings and satin shoes to match. Dorothy was a bewitching little vision in pink, and Peter a cherub in black velvet. Oswald, having reached the stage of real gentleman's evening-dress, required the whole family to assist him in the due arrangement of his tie, over which he was more than usually particular. Ulyth even suspected him of having tried to shave, though he denied the accusation fiercely.

It is always a solemn occasion waiting in the drawing-room listening for the first peal of the bell announcing visitors. Mrs. Stanton was giving a last touch to the flowers, Ulyth sat wielding her new fan (a Christmas present), Oswald was buttoning his gloves. Dorothy, too excited to stand still for a moment, flitted about like a pink fairy.

"I'm to stop up half an hour later than Peter, Rona; do you hear that?" she chattered. "Oh, I do hope the Prestons will arrive first of anybody! I want to dance with Willie. Father let me have a cracker just now, and it's got a whistle inside it. I wish I had a pocket. Where shall I put it to keep it safe? Oh, I know—inside that vase!"

As she spoke, Dorothy jumped lightly on to the seat of the

cosy corner that abutted on the fireplace, and reached upwards to drop her whistle inside the ornament. In her excitement she slipped, tried to save herself, lost her footing, and fell sideways over the curb on to the hearth. Her thin, flimsy dress was within half an inch of the fire, but at that instant Rona, who was standing by, clutched her and pulled her forwards. It all happened in three seconds. She was safe before her father had time to run across the room. The family stared aghast.

"Whew! That was a near shave!" gasped Oswald.

Dorothy, too much surprised and frightened to cry, was clinging to her mother. Mr. Stanton, acting on the spur of the moment, rushed to the telephone to try if any ironmonger's shop in the town was still open, and could immediately send up a wire-gauze fire-protector. The fireplaces in all the other rooms were well guarded, but in the drawing-room the hearth was so wide, and the curb so high, that the precaution had not been considered necessary.

"It only shows how absolutely vital it is to leave no chance of an accident," said Mr. Stanton, returning from the telephone. "Matthews are sending a boy up at once with a guard. If it hadn't been for Rona's promptitude—Oh, there's the bell! Oswald, fetch your mother a glass of water."

Poor Mrs. Stanton looked very pale, but had recovered her composure sufficiently to receive her young guests by the time they were ushered into the drawing-room. Dorothy, child-like, forgot her fright in the pleasure of welcoming her friends the Prestons, and everything went on as if the accident had not occurred. Mr. Stanton, indeed, kept a close watch all the evening, to see that guards were not pushed aside from the fires, and Mrs. Stanton's eyes watched with more than usual solicitude a certain little pink figure as it went dancing round the room. The visitors knew nothing of the accident that had been avoided, and there was no check on the mirth of the party. The guests were of all ages, from Peter's kindergarten comrades to girls who were nearly grown-up, but it was really all the jollier for the mixture. Tall and short danced together with a happy disregard of inches, and even a thorough enjoyment of the disparity. Rona spent a royal evening. Her host and hostess had been kindness itself before, but to-night it seemed as if they conspired together to give her the best of everything. She had her pick of partners, the place of honour at supper, and—by most egregious cheating—the ring somehow tumbled on to her plate out of the trifle.

"I'm getting spoilt," she said to Oswald.

"The mater's ready to kiss your boots," he returned. "I never saw anything so quick as the way you snatched old Dolly."

All good things come to an end some time, even holidays, and one morning towards the end of January witnessed a taxi at the door, and various bags and packages, labelled Llangarmon Junction, stowed inside.

"I don't know how to thank you. I haven't any words," gulped Rona, as she hugged "Motherkins" good-bye.

"Do your best at school, and remember certain little things we talked about," whispered Mrs. Stanton, kissing her. "We shall expect to see you here again."

CHAPTER VIII

THE "STUNT"

The general verdict on Rona, when she arrived back at The Woodlands, was that she was wonderfully improved.

"It isn't only her dresses," said Gertrude Oliver, "though she looks a different girl in her new clothes; her whole style's altered. She used to be so fearfully loud. She's really toned down in the most amazing fashion. I couldn't have believed it possible."

"I'm afraid it's only a veneer," declared Stephanie, with a slighting little laugh. "You'll find plenty of raw backwoods underneath, ready to crop up when she's off her guard. You should have heard her this morning."

"And she broke an ink-bottle," added Beth Broadway.

"Well, she's not perfect yet, of course, but I stick to it that she's improved."

"Oh, I dare say! But Ulyth's welcome to keep her cub. She'll always be more or less of a trial. What else can you expect? 'What's bred in the bone will come out!'"

Angela Brazil

"Yes, I'm a great believer in heredity," urged Beth, taking up the cudgels for her chum. "If you have ancestors it gives you a decided pull."

"Everybody has ancestors, you goose," corrected Gertrude.

"Well, of course I mean aristocratic ones. The others don't count. It must make a difference whether your grandfather was a gentleman or a farm-boy. Rona says herself she's a democrat. I'm sure she looked the part when she arrived."

"I don't know that she exactly looks it now, though," said Gertrude, championing Rona for once.

Everyone at the school realized that the Cuckoo was trying to behave herself. The struggles towards perfection were sometimes almost pathetic, though the girls mostly viewed them from the humorous side. She would sit up suddenly, bolt upright, at the tea table, if Miss Bowes' eye suggested that she was lolling; she apologized for accidents at which she had laughed before, and she corrected herself if a backwoods expression escaped her.

"Am I really any shakes smarter—I mean, more toned up— than I was?" she asked Ulyth anxiously.

"You're far better than you were last term. Do go on trying, that's all!"

"Will they take me as a candidate in the Camp-fire League?"

"I expect so, but we shall have to ask Mrs. Arnold about that."

Since the great reunion by the stream in September there had been no meetings of the Camp-fire League. Mrs. Arnold had been ill, and then had gone away to recruit her health, and no one was able to take her place as "Guardian of the Fire". She was recovered now, and at home again, and had promised to help to make up for lost time by superintending a gathering at the beginning of the new term. It was to be held in the big hall of the school, though the girls begged hard to have it out-of-doors, pleading that on a fine evening they could keep perfectly warm, and it would only resemble a Fifth of November affair.

"That may be all very well for you, but I'm not going to risk Mrs. Arnold's catching cold," returned Miss Bowes; which argument put a final stop to the idea.

"We'll have ripping fun in the hall, if we can't be outside," beamed Addie. "I always enjoy a stunt."

"What's a stunt?" asked Rona.

"A stunt? Why, it's just a stunt!"

"It's an American word," explained Lizzie. "It means just having any fun that comes. An impromptu kind of thing, you know. We sing, or recite, or act, or dance, on the spur of the moment—anything to keep the ball rolling, and anybody may be called upon at any moment to stand up and perform."

"Without knowing beforehand?" queried Rona, looking horror-stricken.

"Yes, that's the fun of it. We have a bag with all our names written on slips of paper, and we draw them out one by one to fill up the programme. Nobody knows who's to come next. You may be the very first, or you may sit quaking all the evening, and never be called at all."

"I hope to goodness—I mean, I hope very much—I shan't be drawn."

"You never know; so you'd better have something in your mind's eye."

Punctually at six o'clock on the appointed night the whole school filed into the hall, each girl carrying a candle in a candlestick. Saluting their leader, they ranged themselves round the room for the opening ceremony. At an indoor meeting this was of necessity different from the kindling of the camp-fire, but it had a certain impressiveness of its own. First the lamps were extinguished, and the room was placed in entire darkness. Then Mrs. Arnold struck a match and lighted her candle, which she held towards the Torch-bearer of highest rank, who lighted hers from it, and performed the same service for her next neighbour. In this way, one after another, the candles were lighted all round the room, every girl saying, as she offered the flame to her comrade: "I pass on my light!" After the "shining" song was sung, all the candlesticks were arranged on the large central table, taking the place the camp-fire would have occupied out-of-doors.

The business of the meeting came first, the roll-call was read, and the recorders gave their reports of the last gathering. Several members were awarded honours for knowing the stars, being able to observe certain things in geology and field botany, or for ability in outdoor sports or indoor occupations, such as carpentry, stencilling, or sewing. The ambulance work and the knitting done last term were specially noted and commended. A few new candidates applied for enrolment, and their qualifications were carefully considered by the Guardian of the Fire. Rona, after undergoing the League Catechism from Catherine Sullivan, the head girl and chief Torch-bearer, had submitted her name as candidate, and now waited with much anxiety to hear whether she would be accepted. After several others had been admitted, Mrs. Arnold at last called:

"Corona Margarita Mitchell."

Quite startled at the unaccustomed sound of her full Christian name, Rona saluted and stepped forward.

"You have passed only three out of the seven tests required," said Mrs. Arnold. "I'm afraid you will have to try again, Rona, and see if you can be more successful before the next meeting. No candidate can be accepted except on very good grounds. That is the law of the League."

Much crestfallen, the Cuckoo fell back into her place, and Mrs. Arnold was just about to read the next name when Ulyth interrupted:

"Please, Guardian, if a candidate has shown unusual presence of mind, may that not stand in place of some of the other tests?"

"It depends on the circumstances. How does that apply in this case?"

"Rona has saved a life," declared Ulyth, then explained briefly how Dorothy had fallen on to the hearth and had been caught back from the fire in the very nick of time.

"In her thin dress she would probably have been burnt to death but for Rona's quickness," added Ulyth, with a tremble in her voice.

"I had not heard of this," replied Mrs. Arnold. "Rona is very greatly to be congratulated on her presence of mind. Yes, I may safely say that it can cancel the tests in which she has failed, and that we may enrol her to-night as a candidate. Corona Margarita Mitchell, if for three months you preserve a good character in the school, and learn to recite the seven rules of the Camp-fire Law, you may then present yourself as eligible for the initial rank of Wood-gatherer in the League. There is your Candidate's Badge."

Immensely gratified, Rona received her little bow of blue ribbon. She had hardly dared to hope for success, as Catherine had been rather withering over her Catechism, and had warned her that she would probably be disqualified. It was pleasant to meet with encouragement, and especially to be commended before the whole school. She had never dreamt of such luck, and she looked her grateful thanks at Ulyth across the room.

She was the last but one on the list of applicants, and when Jessie Howard (alas, poor Jessie!) had been rejected the ceremonial part of the meeting was over. The girls smiled, for now the "stunt" was to begin. Catherine produced the bag, shook it well, and handed it to Mrs. Arnold, who drew out a slip of paper.

"Marjorie Earnshaw!" she announced.

"Glad it's one of the Sixth to open the ball," murmured some of the younger girls as Marjorie stepped to the circle reserved for performers in front of the table.

The owner of the one guitar in the school was always much in request at Camp-fire gatherings, so it seemed a fortunate chance that her name should be drawn first. She had brought her instrument, so as to be prepared in case the lot fell on her, and giving the E string a last hurried tuning she sat down and began a popular American ditty. It was a favourite among the girls, for it had a lively, rollicking chorus, which they sang with great gusto. Fifty voices roaring out: "Don't forget your Dinah!" seemed to break the ice and set the fun going.

Marjorie's E string snapped suddenly, but she played as best she could on the others, though she confessed afterwards that she felt like a horse that has lost its shoe. Except for this accident she would have responded to the enthusiastic calls of "Encore!"; as it was, she retired into the background to fix a new string. It lent a decided element of excitement to the programme that nobody knew what the next item was to be. The lot, as it happened, fell on one of the younger girls, who was overwhelmed with shyness and could only with great urging be persuaded to recite a short piece of poetry. By the law of the Stunt everybody was obliged to perform if called upon, so Aveline fired off her sixteen lines of Longfellow with breathless speed, and fled back joyfully to the ranks of the Juniors. Two piano solos and a step-dance followed, then the turn came to Doris Deane, a member of the Upper Fifth. Doris's speciality was acting, so she promptly begged for two assistants, and chose from IV B a couple of junior members who had practised with her before. Taking Nellie and Trissie for "Asia" and "Australia", she gave the scene from *Mrs. Wiggs of the Cabbage Patch* where that delightful but haphazard heroine gets herself and the children ready to go to the opera. The zeal with which she ironed their dresses, her alternate scoldings and cajolings, her wild hunt for the tickets, which all the while were stuck in her belt, the grandeur of her deportment when the family was at last prepared for the outing, all were most amusingly represented. Doris was really a born actress, and so completely carried her audience with her that the lack of costumes and scenery was not felt in the force of the reality that she managed to throw into her part. Covered with glory, she gave place to her successor, who, while bewailing the hardness of her luck in having to follow so smart a performance, recited a humorous ballad which won peals of applause. Mrs. Arnold again dipped her hand into the bag and unfolded a twist of paper.

"Corona M. Mitchell," she read.

"Not me, surely! I can't do anything," objected Rona hastily.

"You'll have to," laughed the girls. "No one's let off."

"I can't, I tell you. I've no parlour tricks."

"Give us a story, Rona," suggested Ulyth. "One of those New Zealand adventures you used to tell to Peter and Dorothy. They loved them."

"Yes, yes! A camp-fire story. That would be spiffing!" clamoured the girls. "Sit on the floor, near the fire, and we'll all squat near you. We haven't had a story for ages and ages!"

"Tell it just as you did at home," urged Ulyth.

"I'll try my best," sighed Rona, taking a small stool near the fire, so as to be slightly above the audience clustered round the hearthrug.

"It happened about a year ago," she began; "that's summer-time in New Zealand, you know, because the seasons are just opposite. It was Pamela Higson's birthday, and I'd been asked to go over for the day. I saddled Brownie, my best pony, and started at seven, because it's a twelve-mile ride to the Higsons' farm, and I wanted to be early so as to have time for plenty of fun. Brownie was fresh, and he wasn't tired when I got there, so we decided to give him an hour's rest and then ride up into the bush and have a picnic. Pamela showed me her birthday presents while we waited. She'd had a box sent her by the mail, and she was very delighted about it.

"Well, at perhaps eleven o'clock I set off with Pamela and the rest of the Higson children. There was Jake, just my own age, and Billy, a little younger, and Connie and Minnie, the two smallest. Oh yes, we each had our own horse or pony: Everybody rides out there. We slung baskets and tin cans over our saddles and then started up by the dry bed of the river towards the head of the gully. It was very hot (January's like July here), but we all had big hats and we didn't care. It was such fun to be together. When your nearest neighbours are twelve miles off you don't see them often enough to get tired of them. Billy was always making jokes, and Jake was jolly too in a quiet kind of way. Sometimes we could all ride abreast, and sometimes we had to go in single file, and our horses seemed to enjoy it as much as we did. Brownie loved company, so it was a treat for him as well as for me. The place we were going to was a piece of high land that lay at the top of the valley above the Higsons' block. There were generally plenty of berries up there, and we thought they'd just be ripe. It took us a fairly long time to do the climb, because there was no proper road, only a rough track. It was lovely, though, when we got up; we had a splendid view down the gully, and the air was so much cooler and fresher than it had been at the farm. We tethered our horses and gathered scrub to make a fire and boil our kettle. In New Zealand no one thinks of having a meal without drinking tea with it. We'd the jolliest picnic. The Higsons were famous for their cakes, and they'd brought plenty with them. I can tell you we didn't leave very many in the baskets.

"'Best put out our camp-fire,' Jake said when we'd finished; so we all set to work and stamped it out carefully. Everything was so dry with the heat that a spark might easily have set fire to the bush. Then we took our cans and went off to find berries. There were heaps of them; so we just picked and picked and picked for ever so long. Suddenly, when we were talking, we heard a noise and looked round. There was a stampede among the horses, and two of them, Billy's and Connie's, had broken loose and were careering down the gully. We ran as quick as lightning to the others for fear they might also free themselves and follow. I caught Brownie by the bridle and soothed him as well as I could; but he was very excited and trembling, and kept sniffing. Then I saw what had frightened him, for a puff of wind brought a puff of smoke with it, and ahead of us I saw a dark column whirl up towards the sky. Even the youngest child who's lived in the bush knows what that means. When all the grass and everything is so dry, the least thing will start a fire. Sometimes campers-out are careless, and the wind blows sparks; sometimes even a piece of an old bottle left lying about will act as a burning-glass. We didn't inquire the reason; all we knew was that we must tear back to the farm as rapidly as we could. Bush fires spread fearfully fast, and this one would probably sweep straight down the gorge.

"With two animals gone, luck was against us. Billy took Minnie's pony, Connie mounted behind Jake, and I made Minnie come with me on Brownie, because he was so strong, and better able to bear the double burden than Pamela's horse. It was well for us we were good riders, for we pelted down that gully fit to break our necks. Brownie was a sure-footed little beast, but the way he went slithering over rocks would have scared me if I hadn't been more afraid of the fire behind. We knew it would be touch and go whether we could save the farm or not. If the men were all far away there would be very little chance, though we meant to do our level best.

"Well, as I was saying, we just stampeded down the gully, and our horses kept their feet somehow. I guess we arrived at the house like a tornado. We yelled out our news, and coo-eed to some of the men we could see working in the distance. They came running at once, and Mrs. Higson sent up the rocket that was used on the farm as a danger-signal. Fortunately the rest of the men had only gone a short way. They were back almost directly, and everybody set to work to make a wide ring of bare land round the farm. They cut down trees, and threw up earth, and burnt a great patch of grass, and we children helped too for all we were worth. We were only just in time. We could see the great cloud of smoke coming down the valley, and as it grew nearer we heard the roaring or the fire. It seemed to bear down on us suddenly in a great burning sheet. For a moment or two the air was so hot that we could scarcely breathe, then the flame struck our ring of bare land, and parted in two and passed on either side of us, leaving the farm as an island. We watched it go crackling farther down the valley, till at last it spent itself in a rocky creek where it had nothing to feed on. All the place it had passed over was burnt to cinders, a horrible black mass. Only the house and the buildings and a few fields round them were untouched. It was an awful birthday for poor Pamela."

"Was your own farm hurt?" asked the girls breathlessly, as Rona paused in her story.

"Not at all. You see it was in quite a different valley, and the fire hadn't been near. Jake rode home with me, to make sure I was safe. Dad hadn't even seen the smoke."

"Suppose you hadn't noticed the fire when you were up in the hills?"

"Then we should have been burnt to cinders, farm and all."

"I think Rona's most thrilling adventure will have to end our Stunt," said Mrs. Arnold. "It's nearly eight o'clock. Time to wind up and get ready for supper. Attention, please! Each girl take her candle. Where's our pianist? Torch-bearer Catherine, will you start the Good-night Song?"

"I'm a candidate now, thanks to you!" exulted Rona to Ulyth; "perhaps by Easter I may be a Wood-gatherer!"

"It's something to work for, isn't it?" said Mrs. Arnold, who happened to overhear.

CHAPTER IX

A JANUARY PICNIC

Winter in the Craigwen Valley, instead of proving a dreary season of frost or fog, was apt to be as variable as April. Sheltered by the tall mountains, the climate was mild, and though snow would lie on the peaks of Penllwyd and Cwm Dinas it rarely rested on the lower levels. Very early in January the garden at The Woodlands could boast brave clumps of snowdrops and polyanthus, a venturous wallflower or two, and quite a show of yellow jessamine over the south porch. The glade by the stream never seemed to feel the touch of winter. Many of the oak-trees kept their brown leaves till the new ones came to replace them, honeysuckle trails and brambles continually put out verdant shoots, the lastrea ferns that grew near the brink of the water showed tall green fronds untouched by frost, and the moss was never more vivid. The glen, indeed, had a special beauty in winter-time, for the bare boughs of the alders took exquisite tender shades of purples and greys, warming into amber in the sunshine, and defying the cunningest brush which artist could wield to do them justice. By the middle of January the tightly rolled lambs' tails on the hazels were unfolding themselves and beginning to scatter pollen, and a few stray specimens of last summer's flowers, a belated campion or hawkweed, would struggle out from the rough

Angela Brazil

grass under a protecting gorse-bush. The days varied: rain, the penalty for living near mountains, often swept down the valley, bringing glorious cloud-effects, and sending the stream swirling over its boulders with a boom of myriad voices. Sometimes the sudden swelling of its tributaries made the Craigwen River overtop its banks, flooding the low-lying meadows till, augmented by the high tide, its waters filled the valley from end to end like a lake. This occasional flooding of the marsh was good for the fields, and ensured a rich hay-crop next summer, so the school felt it could enjoy the picturesque aspect without needing to deplore loss to the farmers.

On the 21st of January Miss Teddington had a birthday. She would have suppressed the fact altogether if possible, or treated it in quite a surreptitious and off-hand fashion, but with her autograph plainly written in forty-nine separate birthday-books the Fates were against her. She was obliged to receive the united congratulations of the school, to accept, with feigned surprise, the present which was offered her, and to say a few appropriate words of appreciation and thanks. She did not do it well, for her manner was always abrupt, and even verged on the ungracious, the greatest contrast to the bland and tactful utterances of Miss Bowes.

This year the annual ceremony was gone through as usual: Catherine, as head girl, proffered the good wishes and the volume of Carlyle; Lucy Morris, on behalf of the Nature Study Union, handed a bouquet of polyanthus, rosemary, periwinkle, pansies, and pink daisies culled from the garden, the earliness of which Miss Teddington remarked upon, as though she had not watched their progress for the last week.

"I'm very much obliged to you all," she said jerkily, looking nevertheless as if she were longing to bolt for the door.

But she was not yet to make her escape. There was another time-honoured ceremony to be observed. All eyes were turned to Miss Bowes, who rose as usual to the occasion.

"I think, girls," she said pleasantly, "that, considering it is Miss Teddington's birthday, we ought to take some special notice of the occasion. Suppose we ask her to grant a holiday, so that we may make an expedition in her honour. Who votes for this?"

Forty-nine hands were instantly raised, and forty-nine voices cried "I do!" Miss Teddington, who utterly disapproved of odd holidays during term-time, submitted with what grace she could muster, and gave a rather chilly assent, which was immediately drowned in a storm of clapping. The girls, who always suspected the Principals of an annual argument on the subject, felt they had scored for this year at any rate, and were certainly one holiday to the good.

There was no question at all as to where they should walk. Every 21st January, weather permitting, they turned their steps in the same direction. On certain portions of the marsh, near the river, grew fields of wild snowdrops, and to go snowdropping before February set in was as much an institution as turning their money when they first heard the cuckoo, or wishing at the sight of the earliest white butterfly. As a matter of fact, though the delicate fiction of asking for the holiday was preserved, it was such a *sine qua non* that the cook was prepared for it. She had baked jam tartlets and made potted meat the day before, and was already cutting sandwiches and packing them in greaseproof paper. Every girl at The Woodlands possessed a basket, just as she owned a penknife or a French dictionary. It was equally indispensable. She would carry out her lunch in it, and bring it back filled with flowers, berries, or nature specimens, as the case might be. Each was labelled with the owner's name, and hung in a big cupboard under the stairs. Some of the girls also used walking-sticks with crooked handles, which were found convenient weapons for hooking down brambles or branches of catkins.

Shortly after ten o'clock the school started, every Woodlander bearing her basket, containing sandwiches, two tartlets, an orange, and a small enamelled drinking-mug. There were to be no camp-fires to-day, so cold water from the stream would have to suffice, and would make tea all the more welcome when they returned home. It was quite a fine morning, with sudden gleams of sunshine that burst from the clouds and spread in long, slanting, golden rays over the valley; just the kind of sky the early masters of landscape painting loved to put in their pictures, with a background of neutral tint and a bright, scraped-out light in the foreground. The little solitary farms stood out white here and there against the green of the fields, the pine-trees on the hill-sides showed darkly in contrast to the bare larches. Cwm Dinas was inky purple to-day, but Penllwyd was capped with snow. Miss Bowes, who was not a good walker, had not ventured to join the expedition, but Miss Teddington strode along at the head of the party, chatting to some of the Sixth Form.

"I'm sure she's wishing she were giving a Latin lesson instead," said Lizzie Lonsdale. "She looks rather grim."

"Perhaps she's remembering she's a year older to-day," returned Beth Broadway.

"How old is she, do you think?" giggled Addie Knighton.

"That, my child, is a secret that will never be divulged. I dare say you'd like to know?"

"I should, immensely."

"Then you won't be gratified, unless you go to Somerset House and hunt her name up in the register of births. Even then you'd find it difficult, for you don't know her Christian name, only her initial."

"Yes; she never will write more than 'M. Teddington' in anybody's birthday-book. M might stand for Mary or Martha or Margaret or Millicent or anything. Doesn't even Miss Bowes know?"

"If she does she won't tell. It's a state-secret."

"Well, never mind; we call her Teddie, and that will do."

Many were the ingenious devices which the girls had adopted for trying to find out both Miss Teddington's Christian name and her age. They spoke of historic events that had happened before their parents had been born, fondly hoping she might betray some memory of them and commit herself. But she was not to be caught; she treated all events, however recent or old, from a purely impersonal standpoint, and left them still in the dark as to whether she was an infant in arms at the time or an adult able to enjoy the newspapers. On the subject of names she was indifferent, and would express no opinion on the relative merits of Mary, Martha, Margaret, Millicent, Marion, Muriel, Mona, or Maud.

"It's either plain Mary, or something so fearfully fancy she won't own up to it," decided the girls.

In whatever decade Miss Teddington's birthday placed her, this year she was certainly in the prime of life and energy as concerned the school. Her keen eyes noticed everything, and woe betide the slacker who thought to escape her, and dared bring an unprepared lesson to class. Her sarcasms on such occasions made her victims writhe, though they were apt to

Angela Brazil

be witty enough to amuse the rest of the form. Though, like John Gilpin's wife, she was on pleasure bent to-day, she never for a moment forgot she was in charge, and kept turning to see that everybody was following, and nobody straggling far off in the rear.

It was a three-mile walk from The Woodlands to the snowdrop meadows—first along the high road, with an occasional short cut across a field or through a spinney, then down a deep, narrow lane past a farm, where the sight of a new-born lamb (the first of the season) caused great excitement. Some of the girls, who loved old superstitions, pretended to divine their luck by whether it was standing facing them or otherwise when they first caught a glimpse of it; but, the general verdict deciding that it was exactly sideways, they found it impossible to give any accurate predictions for the future.

"You'd better keep to something vague that can be construed two ways, like the Delphic Oracle or *Old Moore's Almanac*," laughed Ulyth.

Once past the farm the walk began to grow specially interesting. The deep lane, only intended for use in summer, when carts brought loads of hay from the marsh, was turned by winter rains into the bed of a stream. The girls picked their way at first along the bank, then by jumping from stone to stone, but finally the water grew so deep it was impossible to proceed farther without wading. They had been in the same emergency before, so it did not daunt their enthusiasm. One and all they scaled the high, wide, loosely built wall to their left. Here they could walk as on a terrace, with the flooded lane on one side and on the other the rushing Porth Powys stream, making its hurrying way to join the Craigwen River. It was not at all an easy progress, for the wall was overgrown with hazel bushes and a tangle of brambles, and its unmortared surface had deep holes, into which the unwary might put a foot. For several hundred yards they struggled on, decidedly to the detriment of their clothing, and rather encumbered by their baskets; then at last they reached the particular corner they were seeking, and scrambled down into the meadow.

This field was such a favourite with the girls that they had come to regard it almost as their own property. Miss Teddington had found it out many years ago, and its discovery was always considered a point in her roll of merit. It was an expanse of grassy land, bounded on one side by the Porth Powys stream and on the other by a deep dyke, and leading down over a rushy tract to the reed-grown banks of the river. The view over the many miles of marshland, with the blue mountains rising up behind and the silvery gleam of the river, was superb. The brown, quivering, feathery reeds made a glorious foreground for the amber and vivid green of the banks farther on; and the gorgeous sky effects of rolling clouds, glinting sun, and patches of bluest heaven were like the beginning of one of St. John's visions.

Near at hand, dotted all over the field, bloomed the wild snowdrops in utmost profusion, with a looser habit of growth, a longer stalk, and a wider flower than the garden variety. Lovely pure-white blossoms, with their tiny green markings, they stood like fairy bells among the grass, so dainty and perfect, it seemed almost a sacrilege to disturb them. The girls, however, were not troubled with any such scruples, and set to work to pick in hot haste.

"I'm going down by the stream," said Ulyth; "one gets far the best there if one hunts about, and I brought my stick."

Rona, Addie and Lizzie joined her, and with considerable difficulty scrambled down to the water's edge. For those who preferred quality to quantity, and who did not mind getting torn by briers, this was undoubtedly the place to come. In pockets of fine river-sand, their roots stretching into the stream, grew the very biggest and finest of the snowdrops. Most of them peeped through a very tangle of brambles; but who minded scratched arms and torn sleeves to secure such treasures?

"Look at these. The stalks must be nine inches long, and the flower's nearly as big as a Lent lily," exulted Ulyth. "I shall send them to Mother, with some hazel catkins and some lovely moss."

"Everybody will be sending away boxes to-night," said Addie. "The postman will have a load."

"What's that?" cried Lizzie, for a sudden rush and scuffle sounded on the other side of the stream, a rat leaped wildly from the bank, and a shaved poodle half jumped, half fell after it into the water.

The rat was gone in an eighth of a second, but the dog found himself in difficulties. It was a case of "look before you leap", and a fat, wheezy, French poodle is not at home in a quick-rushing stream.

"Oh, the poor little beast's drowning!" exclaimed Ulyth in horror.

Rona, with extreme promptitude, had flown to the rescue. Close by where they stood the trunk of a half-fallen alder stretched out over the water. It was green and slippery, and anything but an inviting bridge, but she crawled along it somehow, and, clinging with one hand, contrived to reach the dog's collar with the other and hold him up. What she would have done next it is impossible to say, for he was too heavy to lift in her already precarious position; but at that moment a gentleman, evidently in quest of his pet, parted the hazel boughs and took in the situation at a glance.

"Hold hard a moment," he called, and, scrambling down the bank, managed to make a long arm and hook his stick into the poodle's collar and drag the almost strangled creature to shore.

Until Rona had cautiously wriggled round on the bough, and crept back safely, the spectators watched in considerable anxiety. They need not have been alarmed, however, for after her many New Zealand experiences she thought this a very poor affair.

The owner of the dog shouted his thanks from the opposite bank of the stream and disappeared behind the high hedge. The whole episode had not taken five minutes.

"Do you know who that was? It was Lord Glyncraig," said Addie in rather awestruck tones.

"Was it? Well, I'm sure I don't care," returned Rona a trifle defiantly. "I'd have saved John Jones's dog quite as readily."

"What a pity he didn't ask your name! He might have invited you to tea at Plas Cafn, then you'd have scored over Stephie no end."

"I'm sure I don't want to go to tea at Plas Cafn, thank you," snapped Rona, rather out of temper.

"But think of the fun of it," persisted Addie. "I only wish they'd ask me."

"They won't ask any of us, so what's the use of talking?" said

Lizzie. "Let's go back to the others; it must be time for lunch."

They found the rest of the girls seated on the wall, as being the driest spot available, and already attacking their packets of sandwiches. Some had even reached the jam-tartlet stage.

"It's a good thing we've each got our own private basket, or there wouldn't be much left for you," shouted Mary Acton. "Where have you been all this while?"

"Consorting with members of the Peerage," said Addie airily. "Oh yes, my dear girl! We've had quite what you might call a confidential talk down by the stream with Lord Glyncraig."

"Not really?" asked Stephanie, pricking up her ears.

"Really and truly! He's not your special property any longer. Rona has quite supplanted you."

"I don't believe it. You're ragging." Stephanie was rather pink and indignant.

"Ask the others, if you want to know."

No one was particularly sorry to take a rest after all the scrambling. The lunch tasted good out-of-doors, and the last tartlet had soon disappeared. Rona, perched on a tree-stump, began her orange, and tossed long yellow strands of peel on to the bank below her.

"Oh, stop that, before Teddie catches you!" urged Ulyth; but she was too late, for Miss Teddington had already spied the offending pieces.

"Who threw those?" she demanded. "Then, Rona Mitchell,

you ought to be ashamed of yourself. Go and pick them up at once, and put them inside your basket. What do you think the field will look like if more than fifty people strew it with orange-peel and sandwich-paper! We don't come here to spoil the beautiful spots we have been enjoying. I should be utterly disgraced if the school behaved like a party of cheap-trippers. Woodlanders ought to respect all natural scenery. I thought you would have learnt that by this time, but it appears you haven't. Don't forget it again."

Much crushed, Rona collected the peel, and, wrapping it carefully in her piece of sandwich-paper, put it in the very bottom of her basket, under a layer of catkins. The girls had brought bobbins of thread with them, and were making their snowdrops into little bunches, with ivy leaves and lambs'-tails from the hazel. A few lucky explorers had even found some palm opening on the sallows. Several had nature notes to contribute. Nellie Barlow and Gladys Broughton had seen a real weasel, and plumed themselves accordingly, till Evie Isherwood capped their story by producing the remains of a last year's chaffinch's nest she had found in a tree.

"If I said I'd seen a snake, should I be believed?" whispered Rona.

"Certainly not. Everyone knows that snakes hibernate; so don't try it on," returned Ulyth, laughing.

"Half-past two. We must be going back at once, girls, or there won't be time to send off your snowdrops," said Miss Teddington. "Pack your baskets and come along."

CHAPTER X

TRESPASSERS BEWARE!

The girls left the snowdrop field with reluctance, though they realized the necessity for hurry. Nearly everyone wished to dispatch her spoils home, and unless the boxes were sent very early to the post-office the chances were that there would not be time for the postmaster to stamp them officially, and that they might languish somewhere in the background of the village shop until next day, and consequently arrive at their destination in an utterly withered condition.

The school scrambled back along the top of the wall, therefore, with what haste the brambles and hazel-bushes allowed them, splashed recklessly among the pools of the flooded lane, and regained the high road with quite record speed. Ulyth, walking with Lizzie Lonsdale, had left Rona in the rear. Rona, owing to her intimacy with Ulyth, tried to tag on to V B, often receiving snubs from some of its members. Her own form-mates were all considerably younger than herself. At first they had teased her shamelessly, but since the Christmas holidays, recognizing that she was gaining a more established position in the school, they had begun to treat her more mercifully. Some of them were really rather jolly children, and though twelve seems young to fourteen, the poor Cuckoo was still a lonely enough bird to welcome any crumbs of friendship thrown in her way.

At the present moment Winnie Fowler and Hattie Goodwin were clinging to her arms, one on either side. Their motives, I fear, were a trifle mixed. They found Rona amusing and liked her company, but also they were tired and found if they dragged a little she would pull them along without remonstrance.

"My shoes are ever so wet," boasted Winnie. "I plumped down deep in the lane, and the water went right through the laces at the top. It squelches as I walk. I feel like a soldier in the trenches."

"I've torn my coat in three places," said Hattie, not to be outdone. "It will be a nice little piece of work for Mrs. Johnson to mend it."

"Glad they don't make us mend our own coats here," grunted Winnie.

"Miss Bowes would be ashamed to see me in it if I did," Hattie chuckled, "but I've knitted a whole sock since Christmas, and turned the heel too. Cuckoo, aren't you tired?"

"Not a scrap," replied Rona, who was stumping along sturdily in spite of her encumbrances.

"Well, I am. I wish it wasn't three miles back."

"It's not more than two as the crow flies."

"But we're not crows, and we can't fly, and there are no aeroplanes to give us a lift. We've got to tramp, tramp, tramp along the hard high road. I begin to sympathize with Tommies on the march."

"Why need we stick to the high road?" said Rona, pausing suddenly. "If we struck across country we'd save a mile or more. Look, The Woodlands is over there, and if we made a beeline for it we'd cut off all that enormous round by Cefn Mawr. Who's game to try?"

"Oh, I am, if we can dodge Teddie!"

"Likewise this child," added Winnie.

"Oh, we'll dodge Teddie right enough! It will be good scouting practice," chuckled Rona. "Sit down on that stone and tie your shoelace, and we'll wait for you while the others go on; then we'll bolt through that gate and over the wall into the next field."

The idea that it was scouting practice lent a vestige of sanction to the proceeding. Winnie took the hint, and adjusted her shoelaces with elaborate care and deliberation.

"Don't be all day over that," said Miss Teddington, who passed by but did not wait.

The moment she was round the corner of the road, and the high hedge screened her from view, the three deserters were through the gate and running across the field. They scaled a wall without much difficulty, and found themselves on a wide gorse-grown pasture. Though they could not now see the chimneys of The Woodlands in the distance, there were other landmarks quite sufficient to guide them. They plodded on cheerfully.

"It would be prime to have our snowdrops all packed up before the others got back," ventured Hattie. "They'd be so surprised. They'd wonder how we'd stolen a march on them."

"If Teddie asks where we were, we can truly say 'at the front'," Winnie giggled.

"You'd better not pick up any nature specimens, though, or she'll want to know 'the exact locality' where you found them."

"Um—yes! That might be awkward. This toadstool shall stay on its native heath, in case it tells tales."

It was rather a fascinating walk, all amongst the gorse-bushes. None of the three had been there before, and instinctively the younger ones left Rona to lead the way. Her bump of locality had been well developed in New Zealand, so she strode on with confidence. But the ground shelved down suddenly, revealing a natural feature upon which they had not counted, a fairly wide brook, running between sandy banks. Here indeed was an obstacle. Winnie and Hattie stared at it with blank faces and groaned.

"We'd forgotten the wretched Llanelwyn stream. What atrocious luck! Don't believe there's the ghost of a bridge anywhere. Shall we have to go back?"

"I'm not going back," declared Rona sturdily. "There must be some way of getting over it some where. Come along and we'll prospect."

"Oh, for the wings of a dove!" sighed Hattie. "Even those of the raggedest sparrow would be welcome."

"Better wish yourself a fish, for you may have to try swimming," grunted Winnie.

Angela Brazil

"I can't swim—not a stroke! You'll suggest I shall jump it next, I suppose. Look here, we shall have to go back. There's nothing else for it. Rona! Corona Mitchell! Corona Margarita! Cuckoo! Where've you gone to?"

"Coo—ee!" came in reply from the distance, and presently Rona appeared beckoning vigorously.

"We're—going—back," shouted Hattie.

"No, no! Come along here."

Anxious to see if she had found any solution of the problem, the others pelted down a slope and joined her.

"Here's our bridge," said Rona proudly, as soon as they rounded the corner.

"That thing!" exclaimed Winnie, looking aghast at the decidedly slim pole, that was fixed across the stream as a cattle bar.

"I'm not a tight-rope dancer, thank you!" sneered Hattie rather indignantly.

"It'll be quite easy," Rona urged.

"Oh, I dare say! You won't find me trying to walk across it, I can tell you."

"I didn't ask you to walk. I'm going to sit on it cross-legged, like a tailor, and shuffle myself over. It's broad enough for that. I'll go first."

"Oh, I daren't! I'd drop in!" wailed the younger ones in chorus.

"Now don't funk. What two sillies you are! It won't be as hard as you think. Just watch me do it."

Fortunately the pole had two great advantages: it was firmly fixed in the bank on either side, so that it did not sway about, and, being the trunk of a fir-tree with the bark still left on, its surface offered some grip. Rona's progress was slow but steady. She worked herself over by a few inches at a time. When she reached the water's edge on the far side she dropped on to a patch of silver sand and hurrahed.

"Buck up, and come along," she yelled lustily.

This was scouting with a vengeance, and more than the others had bargained for; but the stronger will prevailed, and though they shook in their shoes they were persuaded to make the experiment.

"I'm all dithering," panted Hattie, as Winnie pushed her forward to try first.

It was not as bad as she had expected. She was able to cling tightly with hands and knees, and though she had one awful moment in the middle, when she thought she was over-balancing, she reached Rona's outstretched hand in due course.

"You squealed like a pig," said the Cuckoo.

"I thought I was done for. Wouldn't you like to feel how my heart's beating?"

"No, I shouldn't. Don't be affected. Come along, Win. We can't wait all day. I'll fish you out if you tumble in, I promise you. It isn't deep enough to drown you."

With many protestations, Winnie, really very much scared, followed the others' lead, and got along quite successfully till within a foot of the brink; then the sudden mooing of a cow on the bank startled her, and so upset her equilibrium that she splashed into the water, wetting one leg thoroughly.

"Ugh! My shoes were squelchy enough before," she lamented. "You can't think how horrid it is."

"Never mind, you've got across."

"But you might sympathize."

"Haven't time. We shall have to hurry up if we mean to be back before the others."

"Did you think the cow was Teddie calling you?" laughed Hattie, who, having got her own trial over, could afford to jest at other people's misfortunes.

"You'd have jumped yourself. Oh dear, I spilt most of my snowdrops, though I did tie the basket round my neck!"

"Never mind; you can't fish them out of the stream now. I'll give you some of mine. Here, take these," said Rona. "I've nobody to send them to," she added, half to herself, as she climbed the bank.

"Oh, thanks awfully! I always send Mother a big bunch. She looks forward to them. I've brought a cardboard box from home on purpose to pack them in, because the cook runs quite out of starch-boxes. Some of the girls last year had to wrap theirs just in brown paper. If you don't want yours, can you spare me a few more?"

"I'll keep just these to put in my bedroom, and you may have the rest if you like," replied Rona, stalking ahead.

Every now and then the sense of her loneliness smote her. She would probably be the only girl in the school who was not sending flowers away to-night. How different it would be if she had anybody in England who took an interest in her and cared to receive her snowdrops!

"It's no use crying for the moon," she decided, blinking hard lest she should betray symptoms of weakness before her juniors. "When a thing can't be helped it can't, and there's an end of it."

"Cuckoo! Corona Margarita! Do wait for us! You walk like the wind."

"Or as if a bull were chasing you," panted Hattie, overtaking her and claiming a supporting arm. "Do you see where we've got ourselves to? The only way out of this is to go straight through the Glynmaen Wood."

"Well, and why shouldn't we go through the Glynmaen Wood? Is it any different to any other wood?"

"No, only they're horribly particular about trespassing. They stick up all kinds of notices warning people off."

"What rubbish! Why, in New Zealand we go where we like."

"Oh, I dare say, in New Zealand!"

"Look, there's a notice up there," said Winnie, pointing over the hedge to a tree whereon was nailed a weather-stained board bearing the inhospitable legend: "Trespassers Beware".

Rona stared at it quite belligerently.

"I should like to pull it down," she observed. "What right has anybody to try to keep places all to themselves?"

"I suppose it belongs to Lord Glyncraig."

"All the more shame to him then. I shall take a particular pleasure in going, just because he sticks up 'Don't'."

"Suppose we're caught?"

"My blessed babes, you don't suppose I've come all this short cut and scrambled over a pole to be turned back by a trespass notice! Do you want to cross the stream again and trail home by the road?"

"Rather not!"

"Then I'll give you a boost to get over the fence there."

The property was well protected. It took Rona's best efforts to help her companions to scale the high oak boards. When they had all dropped safely to the other side they set off through the trees in the direction they judged would bring them out nearest to The Woodlands.

Three girls in thick shoes do not pass absolutely silently through a wood, especially if they indulge in giggles. Winnie and Hattie, moreover, could never be together without chattering incessantly. For the moment they had forgotten every principle of scouting. In that quiet, secluded spot their shrill voices rang out with extreme clearness. A rabbit or two scuttled away, and a pheasant flew off with a whirr. Presently another and heavier pair of boots might be heard tramping towards them, the bushes parted, and a dour-looking face, with lantern jaws and a stubbly chin, regarded them grimly. The gamekeeper glowered a moment, then growled out:

"What are you three a-doing here?"

"That's our own business," retorted Rona briskly.

"Indeed? Well, it happens to be my business too. You're trespassing, and you know it."

"We're doing no harm."

"Aren't you? I suppose it's nothing to scare every pheasant in the wood. Oh dear no!"

"What nonsense! It was only one," exclaimed Rona, standing up against the bullying tone. "You're making the most unnecessary fuss. What right have you to stop us?"

"More right than you've got to be here. I won't have anybody in these woods, schoolgirls or no schoolgirls, so just you get back the way you came, or—"

"That will do, Jordan," said a voice behind him.

The keeper started, turned, and touched his cap obsequiously.

"Beg pardon, my lord, but the trespassing that goes on here gets past bearing, and wants putting a stop to."

"Very well, I'll settle it myself," and Lord Glyncraig—for it was he—readjusted his glasses and stared reprovingly at the three delinquents.

"Ah! girls from The Woodlands—evidently out of bounds. I shall have to report you to your headmistress, I'm afraid. Your names, please."

"Winnie Fowler," "Hattie Goodwin," murmured two subdued voices.

Rona did not answer at all. She kept her head down and her eyes fixed on the ground.

"It's—it's surely not the same girl who did me such a service this morning on the marsh? Then I must repeat my thanks. Now, look here, you've been up to some mischief, all three of you. Get back to school as quick as you can, and I'll say nothing about it! There! Off you go!"

Without another word the sinners pelted along through the wood, never pausing till they reached the railing and climbed over on to the high road. Here, on free ground, they felt at liberty to express their indignation.

"He's a nasty, horrid old thing to turn us out!" panted Hattie.

"How he looked at you, Rona!" said Winnie. "He stared and stared and stared!"

"Wondering where he'd seen me before, I suppose. I expect the green stains on my coat reminded him. I got them hauling up his precious dog."

"It wasn't with him in the wood."

"Oh, it's sitting by the fire drinking linseed tea! It looked a pampered brute."

"We shall have to scoot to keep clear of Teddie."

"All right. Scooterons-nous. Thank goodness, there's the hedge of The Woodlands! We'll slip in through the little side gate."

The three certainly merited discovery for their misdeeds, but on this occasion they evaded justice; for, as luck would have it, they reached the house just a moment or two before the rest of the school, and Miss Teddington, who was in a hurry to pack her boxes of snowdrops, concluded that they must have been in front with Ulyth and Lizzie, and did not stop to remember that she had left them tying Winnie's shoelace by the roadside. It was seldom that such a palpable lapse escaped her keen eye and even keener comprehension; so they might thank their fortunate stars for their escape. Hattie and Winnie made great capital out of the adventure, and recounted all the details, much exaggerated, to a thrilled audience in IV B.

Rona did not mention the matter to Ulyth. Perhaps, knowing her room-mate's standards, in her heart of hearts she was rather ashamed of it.

CHAPTER XI

RONA RECEIVES NEWS

Ulyth and Lizzie Lonsdale were sitting cosily in the latter's bedroom. It was Shrove Tuesday, and, with perhaps some idea of imitating the Continental habit of keeping carnival, Miss Bowes for that one day relaxed her rule prohibiting sweets, and allowed the school a special indulgence. Needless to say, they availed themselves of it to the fullest extent. Some had boxes of chocolate sent them from home; others visited the village shop and purchased delicacies from the big bottles displayed in the windows; while a favoured few managed to borrow pans from the kitchen and perform some cookery with the aid of friends. Lizzie had been concocting peppermint creams, and she now leant back luxuriously in a basket-chair and handed the box to Ulyth. The two girls were friends, and often met for a chat. Ulyth sometimes wished they could be room-mates. Though Rona was immensely improved, she was still not an entirely congenial companion. Her lack of education and early training made it difficult for her to understand half the things Ulyth wanted to talk about, and it was troublesome always to have to explain. In an equal friendship there must be give and take, and to poor Rona Ulyth was constantly giving her very best, and receiving nothing in return. Lizzie, on the contrary, was inspiring. She played and painted well, was fond of reading, and was ready to help to organize any forward movement in the school. She and Ulyth pottered together over photography, mounted specimens for the museum, tried new stitches in embroidery, and worked at the same patterns in chip carving. The two girls were at about the same level of attainment in most things, for if Ulyth had greater originality, Lizzie was the more steady and plodding. It was Ulyth's failing to take things up very hotly at first, and then grow tired of them. She was apt to have half a dozen unfinished pieces of fancywork on hand, and her locker in the carpentry-room held several ambitious attempts that had never reached fruition.

Lizzie, as she munched her peppermint creams, turned over the pages of a volume of Dryden's poems, and made an occasional note. Each form kept a "Calendar of Quotations" hung up in its classroom, the daily extracts for which were supplied by the girls in rotation. It was Lizzie's turn to provide the gems for the following week, and she was hunting for something suitable.

"I wish Miss Bowes had given me Shakespeare," she said. "I could have got heaps of bits out of my birthday-book, just suitable for the month, too. I don't know why she should have pitched on Dryden. No one's going to be particularly cheered next week with my quotations. I've got:

"'MONDAY

"'When I consider life, 't is all a cheat;
Yet, fooled with hope, men favour the deceit,
Trust on, and think to-morrow will repay;
To-morrow's falser than the former day.'"

"'TUESDAY

Angela Brazil

"'All human things are subject to decay,
And when Fate summons, monarchs must obey.'"

"That's dismal, in all conscience!" put in Ulyth.

"'WEDNESDAY

"'Great wits are sure to madness near allied,
And thin partitions do their bounds divide.'"

"That sounds quite as dismal, does it not? I wonder why Scott calls Dryden 'glorious John'? I think he's rather a dismal poet. Listen to this:

"'In dreams they fearful precipices tread,
Or, shipwrecked, labour to some distant shore,
Or in dark churches walk amongst the dead:
They wake with horror, and dare sleep no more.'"

Shall I put it down for Thursday?"

"For goodness' sake don't! You'll give us all the creeps," laughed Ulyth.

"Well, it won't be a champion week."

"I'll tell you what you might do. Draw some illustrations round the mottoes. That would make them more interesting."

"Oh, I dare say! I haven't time to bother."

"Nonsense, you have! I'll do some of them for you. You needn't be original. It doesn't take long to copy things."

"Will you do four, then, if I do three?"

"All serene. I'll begin this evening if you'll give me the cards."

Ulyth dashed off quite a pretty little pen-and-ink sketch in ten minutes after tea, and put the cards by in her drawer, intending to finish them during "handicraft hour" the next day; but she completely forgot all about them, and never remembered their existence till Saturday, when she came across them by accident, and was much dismayed at her discovery.

"I'll have to do them somehow, or Lizzie'll never forgive me," she ruminated. "I must knock them off just as fast as I can. I could copy those little figures from the *American Gems*; they're in outline, and will be very easy. Oh, bother! It's cataloguing day, and one's not supposed to use the library. What atrocious luck!"

Twice during the term the books of the school library were called in for purposes of review by the librarian, and on those days nobody was allowed to borrow any of the volumes. It was most unfortunate for Ulyth that this special Saturday should be the one devoted by the monitresses to the purpose. She had failed Lizzie so often before in their joint projects that she did not wish to encounter fresh reproaches. Somehow three illustrations had to be provided, and that within the space of about half an hour. Ulyth was fairly clever at drawing, but she was not capable of producing the pictures out of her head. She must obtain a copy, and that quickly.

"Helen Cooper's librarian this month," she thought. "I wonder if she's finished checking the catalogue yet? I saw her walking down the stream five minutes ago with Mabel Hoyle. Why shouldn't I have the *American Gems* for half an hour? It wouldn't do any harm. It really is the merest red tape that we mayn't use the books. I shall just take French leave and borrow it."

Ulyth went at once to the library. Helen had evidently been at work there, for the list lay open, with a sheet of paper near, recording the condition of some of the copies. A glue-pot and some rolls of transparent gummed edging showed that Helen had been busy mending battered covers and torn pages. She probably meant to finish them after tea. The book of American gems was in its usual place on the shelf. The temptation was irresistible. Ulyth did not notice, as she was taking it down, that someone with a smooth head of sleek fair hair was peeping round the corner of the door, and that a pair of not too friendly blue eyes were watching the deed. If flying footsteps whisked along the corridor and out into the garden, she was blissfully unconscious of the fact. She took the volume to her own form-room and settled herself at her desk with her drawing materials, cardboard, pencil, india-rubber, fine pen, and a bottle of Indian ink. The little figures were exactly what she wanted, quite simple in outline, but most effective, and not at all difficult. They would certainly improve Lizzie's calendar for the week, and relieve the sombre character of the Dryden quotations. She worked away very rapidly, sketching them lightly in pencil, intending to finish them in ink afterwards. She grew quite interested, especially when she reached the pen part. That little face with its laughing mouth and aureole of hair was really very pretty; she had copied it without having to use the india-rubber once.

"Ulyth Stanton, what are you doing with that book?" said a voice from behind her desk.

Beside her stood Helen Cooper and Stephanie Radford, the former hugely indignant, the latter with a non-committal expression. Ulyth started so violently that the bottle of Indian ink overturned and spread itself out in three streams.

"Oh Jemima!" shrieked Ulyth in consternation.

"Now you've done it!" exclaimed Helen angrily. "Ink all over the page. What a disgraceful mess! For goodness' sake stop; you're making it worse. Give it to me."

Ulyth, who was frantically mopping up the black streams with her pocket handkerchief, surrendered the book to the outraged librarian. Nemesis had indeed descended upon her guilty head.

"You knew perfectly well that you weren't allowed to take it to-day," scolded Helen. "You sneaked into the library and got it while I was out."

"Someone else has been sneaking too," thought Ulyth, with a glance at Stephanie's face. "I fancy I know who turned informer." Then aloud she said: "I'm fearfully sorry. I'll buy a new copy of the book."

"I don't believe you can; it's one Mrs. Arnold gave to the school, and is published in America. I'll try sponging it with salts of lemon, but I'm afraid nothing will take out the stain. I thought better of you, Ulyth Stanton. One doesn't expect such things from V B. You'll borrow no more books till the end of the month. Do you understand?"

Ulyth responded with what meekness she could muster. She admitted that the monitress had reason for wrath, and that she had really no excuse worthy of urging in extenuation of her crime. It was hard to be debarred the use of the library for more than a fortnight, but, Helen, she knew, would enforce that discipline rigidly. The unfortunate motto-cards had come in for the bulk of the ink, and were completely spoilt. Ulyth carried the ruins to Lizzie's bedroom and pleaded *peccavi*.

"Well, I suppose it can't be helped. I've done my three cards with pictures of flowers, and the rest of the calendar will have to be plain," said Lizzie. "You were rather an idiot, Ulyth."

"I know. I'd have asked Helen for the book if she'd been anywhere near, and I meant to tell her afterwards that I'd taken it."

"Didn't you explain that to her?"

"No. It didn't come well when she'd just caught me."

"You let her think the worst of you."

"It couldn't be helped. I'm sure Stephanie hunted her up and told her."

"Stephanie doesn't like you."

"No, because I champion Rona, and Stephanie can't bear her."

"There's nothing so much wrong with the poor old Cuckoo now; she's wonderfully inoffensive."

"Yes, but she's not aristocratic. Stephie rubs that in to her continually. She calls her 'a daughter of the people'."

"Stephanie Radford can be uncommonly snobbish sometimes."

Stephanie from the very first had resented Rona's presence at

The Woodlands, and since the practical joke which the latter had played upon her she had disliked her heartily. She lost no opportunity of showing her contempt, and of trying to make Rona seem of small account. She revived an ancient tradition of the school which made it a breach of etiquette for girls to go into other form-rooms than their own, thus banishing Rona from V B, where she had often been brought in by Ulyth or good-natured Addie to share the fun that went on. If obliged to take Rona's hand in figure-dancing, she would only give the extreme tips of her fingers, and if forced on any occasion to sit next to her, she would draw away her skirts as if she feared contamination.

"The Woodlands isn't what it used to be," she would assure a select circle of listeners. "When my eldest sister was here there were the Courtenays and the Derringtons and the Vernons and quite a number of girls of really good family. Miss Bowes would never have dreamt then of taking a girl she knew nothing about; she was so particular whom she received."

"The poor old Cuckoo has her points," volunteered Addie. "I'm afraid most of us aren't 'county'!"

"All schools are more mixed than they used to be," admitted Stephanie candidly; "but I'd draw the line at specimens straight from the backwoods."

Few of the girls really liked Stephanie, nevertheless her opinions carried weight. A school-mate who dresses well, talks continually of highborn friends, and "gives herself airs" can nearly always command a certain following among the more unthinking of her comrades, and such girls as Beth Broadway, Alice and Merle Denham, and Mary Acton were easily impressed by Stephanie's attitude of superiority, and ready to follow her lead on a question of caste. It gave them a kind of reflected credit to belong to Stephanie's circle, and they liked to pride themselves upon their exclusiveness.

Though Rona was many thousand miles away from her home, she evidently did not forget her New Zealand friends, and looked out anxiously for the thin foreign letters which arrived from time to time. She never showed them to anybody, and spoke little of old associations, but a word would slip out here and there to reveal that she cared more than she would give her schoolfellows to suppose. One afternoon, shortly before the New Zealand mail was expected, Rona was working in her portion of the garden, when Mary Acton brought her a message.

"Some visitors to see you. They're waiting in the practising-room," announced Mary.

"Visitors to see me!" exclaimed Rona, throwing down her rake. "Whoever can they be?"

"I'm sure I don't know," replied Mary stolidly. "They asked for Miss Mitchell, so I suppose that's you. There isn't anyone else in the school named Mitchell."

"It must be me!"

Rona's eyes were wide with excitement. Visitors for herself! It was such an utter surprise. For one moment a wild idea flashed across her mind. Her face suddenly hardened.

"What are they like? Do you know them?" she gasped.

"Not from Adam, or rather Eve. They're just two very ordinary-looking females."

Much agitated, Rona flew into the house to wash her hands,

slip off her gardening-apron, and change her shoes. When this very hasty toilet was completed, she walked to the practising-room and entered nervously. Two ladies were sitting near the piano, with their backs to the window. They were not fashionably dressed, but perhaps they were cold, for both wore their large coat collars turned up. Their felt hats had wide floppy brims. One carried a guide to North Wales, and the other held an open motor-map in her hand, as if she had been studying the route.

"Miss Mitchell? How d'you do?" said the taller of the two as Rona entered. "I dare say you'll be surprised to see us, and you won't know who we are. I'm Mrs. Grant, and this is my cousin, Miss Smith. We live in New Zealand, and know some of your friends there. We're visiting England at present, and as we found ourselves motoring through North Wales, we thought we would call and see you."

"It's very good of you," faltered Rona. "Which friends of mine do you know?"

"The Higsons. They sent you all kinds of messages."

"Oh! How are they? Do tell me about them!"

Rona's cheeks were flushed and her lips quivering.

"Pamela has grown, of course. Connie and Minnie have had measles. Billy had a fall from his horse and sprained his ankle badly, but he's all right again now."

"And Jake?"

"Spends most of his time with the Johnson girls."

"Who are they? I never heard of them."

"They came after you left."

"To which farm?"

"Oh, not very far away, I believe!"

"I wonder Pamela didn't tell me all that in her letter. Which farm can it possibly be? Surely not Heathlands?"

"I believe that was the name."

"Then have the Marstons gone?"

"Yes, to the North Island."

"Oh! I'm very sorry. Why didn't they write to me? Did you hear any other news, please?"

"Pamela told me something about your home."

A shadow crossed Rona's face.

"Is it—is it Mrs. Barker?" she asked nervously.

"Yes, it's about her."

"What has she been doing?"

"Getting married again."

"Oh! Oh! Who would have her?"

"Your father."

"No!" shrieked Rona, her eyes ablaze. "It can't be! That dreadful, drinking woman! Oh, I can't—I won't believe it!"

"She's your stepmother now, whether you like it or not."

"Daddy! Daddy! It can't be! How could you? You knew she drank!"

"He's drinking himself—like a fish."

"No! My daddy?"

Rona, a moment ago furious, had turned white as a ghost. She put out a trembling hand and clutched the piano blindly; then, with a pitiful, broken cry, she fell, half-fainting, half-sobbing, on to the floor. At that moment Ulyth, with her music-case, entered the room.

"What's the matter? Rona! Rona, dear! Are you ill? Who are these—people?"

She might well ask, for the behaviour of the two strangers was most unprecedented. They were leaning on each other's shoulders and roaring with laughter. One of them suddenly threw up her hat, and turned down her collar, revealing the familiar features of Stephanie Radford.

"Done you brown!" she exploded. "Paid you back in your own coin for your precious Eau de Venus sell! I'm even with you now, Rona Mitchell! Come along, Beth." And the pair disappeared, guffawing.

Rona picked herself up shakily, and subsided on to a chair, with her face in her hands.

"It's not true then?" she quavered.

"What isn't true?"

"They told me Dad had married Mrs. Barker, and that he was—drinking!"

"Stephanie told you that?"

"Yes. Oh, I'm queer still!"

"Rona, darling, of course it's nothing but a black, wicked lie. Don't cry so. There isn't a word of truth about it. They were only ragging you. Oh, don't take it so hard! I'll settle with Stephanie for this."

Half an hour afterwards a very grim, determined Ulyth, supported by Lizzie Lonsdale, sought out the masqueraders and spoke her mind.

"She ragged me, so why shouldn't I turn the tables on her? It's nothing to make such a hullabaloo about!" yapped Stephanie.

"But it is. The trick she played on you was only fun after all. Yours was the cruellest thing you could think of to hurt and wound her. You may pride yourself on your family, Stephanie Radford, but I'm sure the very commonest person would have had nicer feelings than to do this. I can never think the same of you and Beth again."

"Oh, of course you take up the cudgels for your precious Cuckoo!" snapped Stephanie. "Don't make such an absurd fuss. I shall do what I like, without you setting yourself up to lecture me. So there! If you don't like it, you may lump it."

"Not a very aristocratic form of expression for a scion of the Radfords of Stoke Radford!" commented Lizzie, as she and Ulyth stalked away.

CHAPTER XII

SENTRY DUTY

The spring term wore slowly on. March winds came and went, taking the sweet violets with them, but leaving golden Lent lilies and a wealth of primroses as a legacy to April. The larch forest above Porth Powys was a tangle of green tassels, the hedgerows were starry with blackthorn, and the *Pyrus japonica* over the dining-room windows was a mass of rosy blossom. Spring was always a delightful season at The Woodlands; with the longer days came rambles and greater freedom. Popular opinion ran high in extolling country life, and any girl who ventured to prefer town pleasures found herself entirely in the minority.

Rona had several invitations for the Easter holidays, one from Mrs. Stanton among the number; but Miss Bowes, thinking it better for Ulyth to have a rest from her room-mate's presence, decided in favour of Winnie Fowler. Ulyth could not help feeling a sense of relief that the matter was thus settled. Rona was very little trouble to her now—indeed, she rather liked her company; but she would be glad to have her mother to herself for the few short weeks.

"I wouldn't for the world have tried to stop her coming, Motherkins," she wrote home; "but Miss Bowes said most emphatically that she must go to the Fowlers. I'm sure they'll give her a good time, and—well, I admit it will be a rest to me. Just at present I don't want to share you. Now you know the whole of your horrid daughter! Lizzie asked me if I would spend part of the holidays with her, but I managed to make an excuse. I felt I couldn't spare a single precious day away from you. I have so much to talk about and tell you. Am I greedy? But what's the use of having one's own lovely mother if she isn't just one's ownest sometimes? I tell you things I wouldn't tell anyone else on earth. I don't think all the girls feel quite the same; but then their mothers can't possibly be like mine! She's the one in a thousand! I'm sitting up late in my bedroom to write this, and I shall have to report myself to Miss Lodge to-morrow; but I felt I must write."

After the Easter holidays everybody returned to The Woodlands prepared to make the most of the coming term. With the longer evenings more time was allowed out-of-doors, and the glade by the stream became a kind of summer parlour. Those girls who had some slight skill in carpentry constructed rustic benches and tables from the boughs blown down by last autumn's storms, and those who preferred nature untouched by art had their favourite seats in snug corners among the bushes or on the stones by the water-side. With the first burst of warm weather bathing was allowed, and every morning detachments of figures in mackintoshes and tennis-shoes might be seen wending their way towards the large pool to indulge in the exhilarating delight of a dip in clear, flowing water, followed by a brisk run round the glade. These pre-breakfast expeditions were immensely appreciated; the girls willingly got up earlier for the purpose, and anyone who manifested a disposition to remain in bed was denounced as a "slacker".

One day, towards the end of May, when some of the members of V B were sitting with their fancywork on the short grass under an oak-tree, Addie Knighton came from the house and joined them. There was beaming satisfaction in Addie's twinkling grey eyes; she rubbed her hands ostentatiously, and chuckled audibly.

"What's to do, Addie, old girl? You're looking very smug," said Lizzie.

"Aha! Wouldn't you like to know? What'll you give me if I tell you now?"

"Never buy pigs in pokes. It mayn't be important at all," volunteered Merle.

"Oh, indeed! Isn't it? Just wait till you hear."

"It's nothing but one of your sells," yawned Gertrude Oliver, moving so as to rest her back more comfortably against Ulyth.

"Mrs. Arnold doesn't generally spring sells upon us."

Ulyth jumped up so suddenly that Gertrude collapsed with a squeal of protest.

"Mrs. Arnold here and I never knew! Where is she?"

"Don't excite yourself. She's gone by now. She only stayed ten minutes, to see Miss Bowes, but it was ten minutes to some purpose. Do you know what she's actually proposed?"

Addie's listeners were as eager now as they had been languid before.

"Go ahead, can't you?" urged Lizzie.

"Well, the whole school's to go camping for three days."

This indeed was news!

"Stunning!"

"Spiffing!"

"Ripping!"

"Scrumptious!" burst in a chorus from the elated four.

"Details, please," added Ulyth. "When and where, and how, and why?"

"Is it a Camp-fire business?" asked Lizzie.

"Of course it is or Mrs. Arnold wouldn't be getting it up. It's happened this way. The Llangarmon and Elwyn Bay detachments of Boy Scouts are to camp at Llyn Gwynedd for ten days early in June. Mr. Arnold has the arranging of it all. And Mrs. Arnold suggested that the tents might just as easily be hired a few days sooner, and we could use them before the boys came. It's such a splendid opportunity. It would be too expensive to have everything sent down on purpose just for us, but when they're there we can hire the camp for very little extra. It's the carriage and erecting that cost so much. Miss Bowes, I believe, hummed and ha-ed a little, but Teddie just tumbled to the idea and persuaded the Rainbow to clinch it."

"Good old Teddie! I believe it's the tragedy of her life that she can't live altogether in the open air. She adores Red Cross Work."

"The teachers are all to come to camp; they're as excited as you please about it. It was Miss Lodge who told me that Mrs. Arnold was here, and I rushed down the drive and caught her just for a second."

This indeed was an event in the annals of the school. Never since the Camp-fire League was started had its members found any opportunity of sampling life under canvas. They had practised a little camp cookery down by the stream, but their experiments had not gone much farther than frying eggs and bacon or roasting potatoes in hot ashes, and they were yearning to try their hands at gipsies' stews and gallipot soups. With Mrs. Arnold for leader they expected a three days' elysium. Even Miss Teddington, they knew, would rise to the occasion and play trumps. Llyn Gwynedd was a small lonely lake about six miles away, in the heart of the mountains beyond Penllwyd and Glyder Garmon. It was reached from The Woodlands by a track across the moors, but it communicated by high road with Capelcefn station, so that tents, camp-furniture, and provisions could be sent up by a motor-lorry. The ground was hired from a local farmer, who undertook to supply milk, butter, and eggs to the best of his ability, and to bring meat and fresh vegetables from Capelcefn as required. To cater for a whole school up in the wilds is a task from which many Principals would shrink, and Miss Bowes might be forgiven if she had at first demurred at the suggestion. But, with Mr. Arnold's practical experience to help her, she gave her orders and embarked (not without a few tremors) upon the proceeding.

"If the mountain air makes you so hungry you eat up two days' provisions in one, it means you'll have to fast on the third day," she assured the girls. "I'm sending up what I hope will be sufficient. It's like victualling a regiment. Of course we shan't go at all if it's wet."

Mr. Arnold, who very kindly volunteered to see that the

camp was properly set up and in thorough working order before the school took possession, superintended the erection of the tents and reported that all was in apple-pie condition and only waiting for its battalion. On 2nd June, therefore, a very jolly procession started off from The Woodlands. In navy skirts and sports coats, tricolor ties, straw hats, and decorated with numerous badges and small flags, the girls felt like a regiment of female Territorials. Each carried her kit on her back in a home-made knapsack containing her few personal necessities, and knife, spoon, fork, and enamelled tin mug. A band of tin whistles and mouth organs led the way, playing a valiant attempt at "Caller Herrin'". The teachers also were prepared for business. Miss Teddington, who had done climbs in Switzerland, came in orthodox costume with nailed boots and a jaunty Tyrolean hat with a piece of edelweiss stuck in the front. Miss Lodge wore a full-length leather coat and felt hat in which she looked ready to defy a waterspout or a tornado. Miss Moseley, who owned to an ever-present terror of bulls, grasped an iron-spiked walking-stick, and Miss Davis had a First Aid wallet slung across her back. In the girls' opinion Miss Bowes shirked abominably. Instead of venturing on the six-mile walk she had caught the morning train to Capelcefn, and was going to hire a car at the Royal Hotel and drive up to the lake with the provisions. Mrs. Arnold, who, with her husband, had taken rooms at the farm for a few days, was already on the spot, and would be ready to receive the travellers when they arrived.

On the whole it was a glorious morning, though a few ill-omened clouds lingered like a night-cap round Penllwyd. Larks were singing, cuckoos calling, bluebells made the woods seem a reflection of the sky, and the gorse was ablaze on the common. The walk was collar-work at first, up, up, up, climbing a steep track between loose-built, fern-covered walls, taking a short cut over the slope that formed the spur of Cwm Dinas, and scaling the rocky little precipice of Maenceirion. Some who had started at a great rate and with much enthusiasm began to slacken speed, and to realize the wisdom of Miss Teddington's advice and try the slow-going, steady pace she had learned from Swiss guides.

"You can't keep it up if you begin with such a spurt," she assured them. "Alpine climbing has to be like the tortoise— slow and sure."

Once on the plateau beyond Cwm Dinas progress was easier. It was still uphill, but the slope was gentler. They were on the open moors now, following a path, little more than a sheep track, that led under the crag of Glyder Garmon. Except for an occasional tiny whitewashed farm they were far from human habitations, and the only signs of life were the small agile Welsh sheep, the half-wild ponies that grazed on these uplands during the summer months, and a pair of carrion crows that wheeled away, croaking hoarsely at the sight of intruders. On and on over what seemed an interminable reach of coarse grass and whinberry-bushes, jumping tiny brooks, and skirting round sometimes to avoid bogs, for much of the ground was spongy, and though its surface of sphagnum moss looked inviting, it was treacherous in the extreme. At last they had rounded the corner of Glyder Garmon, and there, far away to the right, like a sheet of silver, Llyn Gwynedd lay gleaming in the distance.

The sight of their destination, even though it was two miles away, cheered up those weaker spirits that were beginning to lag, especially as something white on the south side, when examined through Miss Teddington's field-glasses, proved to be the tents. Three-quarters of an hour's brisk walking brought them to the lake, and in ten minutes more they were announcing their approach to the camp in a succession of wild hoorays.

Angela Brazil

Mr. and Mrs. Arnold were waiting to do the honours, and, parading in their very best style, the League marched in and took possession.

By the time they had been two hours at Llyn Gwynedd all the girls felt like old, well-seasoned campers. Mrs. Arnold was no novice, and at once assumed her post as leader and captain in command. Miss Bowes, Miss Teddington, and the other teachers were assigned tents of honour, and every member of the League was placed on definite duty. Some were cooks, some water-carriers, some scullions, and some sentries, according to their qualifications and the rank they held in the League.

The field hired for the camping-ground had been carefully chosen. It was on the far side of the lake, away from the road, sheltered on the north and east by mountain ridges, and with a shelving beach of fine silvery sand where the waves lapped in gentle little ripples. A narrow brook, leaping from the heights above, passed through the centre and gave a quite uncontaminated water supply. All around rose peaks which had not been visible at The Woodlands, the rough, splintered crest of Craig Mawr, the smoother summit of Pencastell, and the almost inaccessible precipice of Carnedd Powys. It was glorious to sit by the lake and feel that they were not obliged to return to school before dark, but could stay and watch the sun set behind Pencastell and the gloaming creep quietly on. Of course everybody wanted to explore the immediate vicinity, and little bands, each in charge of a Torch-bearer, were allowed to skirt round the lake within sight of the camp. Each girl had her League whistle, and knew the signals which meant "Meal-time", "Danger", and "Return instantly to camp". These had been rehearsed in the glade at The Woodlands, and formed part of the examination of every candidate.

Ulyth, as a Torch-bearer, was able to head a party, and

started off in quest of bog myrtle along the bank, returning with great armfuls of the delicious-smelling aromatic shrub to cast into the fire during the evening "stunt".

The gathering of the League that night was a memorable occasion. The ceremonies were observed with strictest formality, and as visitors were present a special welcome song was sung in their honour. The scene was immensely picturesque and romantic: the red sun setting between Craig Mawr and Pencastell threw a last glow on the lake, the blazing fire lighted up the camp and the rows of eager faces, and behind all was the background of the eternal hills.

Rona, having successfully passed through her probation, was admitted as a Wood-gatherer and awarded the white badge of service. Several younger girls also received initiation into membership. With the League ceremonial, songs, stories, and cocoa-making, the evening passed very swiftly away. At nine o'clock everybody was expected to turn in. A night under canvas was a new experience. The stretcher-beds and the clean blankets looked inviting. Strict military discipline was observed in the camp, and sentries were told off on duty. In as perfect order as a regiment the girls went to their tents. Ulyth was sharing quarters with Addie, Lizzie, and Gertrude. She tucked herself up in her blankets, as she had been taught at camp drill, and then lay quietly for a long, long time, watching the patch of sky through the tent door.

She seemed only to have been asleep for about an hour, when the patrol touched her on the shoulder. Instantly she sprang up, broad awake.

"Relieve sentry at west guard," was the order, and the patrol passed on.

It was too dark to see her watch, but Ulyth knew it must be

nearly one o'clock. She hastily donned the warm garments ordered to be worn by sentries, and hurried away to relieve Helen Cooper. Her post was at the west end of the camp, where the field merged into a rushy swamp before it rose into the hill that led towards the farm.

"The password is 'Louvain'," said Helen, retiring, not at all sorry to seek the comfort of her bed. "One leg of the camp-stool is most rickety, so I warn you not to lean too hard on it. Good night."

Left alone, Ulyth sat down with extreme caution on the deficient camp-stool and surveyed the situation. There were clouds across a waning moon, and it was fairly dark. She could see the outlines of the tents in black masses behind her; in front the field lay dim and shadowy, with a mist creeping from the water. Up above, to her right, against an indigo sky, the Great Bear was standing almost on its head, with its tail in the air. One of the tests of a Torch-bearer was a knowledge of the stars, and Ulyth had learnt how to tell the time by the position of this particular constellation. She made a rapid calculation now, reckoning from the day of the month, and was glad to find it came out correctly. Cassiopeia's white arms were hidden by the mountains, but the Milky Way shimmered in the east, and overhead Arcturus blazed as he had done in the days when the patriarch Job recorded his brilliance. To the extreme north a patch of light lay behind Penllwyd, where the sun, at this season hardly dipping far out of sight, worked his course round to the east again. How quiet it was! The silence was almost oppressive. The gentle lap of the tiny waves on the lake was not equal to the rush of the stream at The Woodlands. Not even a night-bird called. The camp was absolutely still and slumbering.

Ulyth rose and paced about for a while. It was too cold to sit still long. She must only use the camp-stool when she needed a rest.

"Sentries ought to be allowed chocolates," she murmured, "or hot peppermints, just to keep up their spirits. Ugh! How weird and eerie it all is! There isn't a sound anywhere. It's not an enlivening performance to keep watch, I must say."

She stopped, suddenly on the alert. What was that noise in the darkness to her left? She distinctly heard a rustle among the gorse-bushes, and thought something moved in the deep shadow.

"Halt! Who goes there?" she challenged.

There was no reply, but the rustle sounded again, this time nearer to the camp. She listened with every sense strained to the uttermost. Something or someone was slinking in from the field and creeping cautiously towards the tents; of that she was nearly certain. Wild ideas of thieving tramps flooded her brain. A louder sound confirmed her suspicions. She could hear it quite distinctly in the direction of the kitchen. Her duty was plain. She blew her whistle promptly; it was answered by those of the three other sentries, from the north, east, and south quarters, and immediately torches began to flash, and voices to ask the cause of alarm. The guard was roused, and began an instant tour of inspection.

"Something crept past me, straight towards the centre of the camp," Ulyth reported.

The lights flashed away in the direction of the kitchen. The girls were on their mettle, and meant business. Whoever the intruder was, he should be run to earth and made to give an account of himself. They felt perfectly capable of taking him prisoner and binding his hands behind him with a rope.

Indeed, they thought they should hugely enjoy doing so, particularly if he turned out to be a burglar. Numbers give courage, and a very martial spirit was in the air.

"If he's hiding in one of the tents we'll drag him out by the legs!" proclaimed Marjorie Earnshaw fiercely.

Everybody was sure it must be a "he". The news spread through the camp like lightning, and it was even rumoured that he wore a coat and top-boots. Miss Teddington herself had emerged, and was waving a lantern as a searchlight.

"This way," blustered Marjorie, heading for the kitchen quarter. "The sneaking cur! We'll have him!"

"Why aren't we allowed bayonets?" lamented Ruth White.

"Oh, I hear a noise! There's something there really," urged Kathleen Simpson, with a most unsoldierly squeal. "Oh, I say! Here he comes!"

There was a sudden scratch and scramble, and from out the larder rushed a dark object on four legs, with a white something in its mouth. Helen made a valiant dash at it, but it dodged her, and flew like the wind away between the tents and off somewhere over the fields in the direction of the farm. The guard with one accord burst out laughing.

"A thieving Welsh sheep-dog raiding the larder!" exclaimed Catherine.

"It's stolen a whole leg of mutton, the brute!" wailed Doris, who belonged to the Commissariat Department. "I didn't think it could have reached that. It must have jumped high. It doesn't deserve its prize."

"No wonder it wouldn't answer when I challenged it," observed Ulyth.

"Well, I'm glad it's no worse than a dog," said Miss Teddington. "We must take steps to-morrow to make the larder safer, or we shall be troubled again."

"We'll place a guard over it," replied Catherine promptly. "Jessie Morrison, you are on sentry duty at once to watch the larder. Maggie Orton will relieve you at three."

CHAPTER XIII

UNDER CANVAS

After the scare in the small hours, everyone settled down again to slumber. Nevertheless the girls woke with the birds. Many of them had registered a solemn vow the night before that they would watch the sun rise, and each was pledged to arouse the others at all costs; so at the first hint of dawn heads began to pop out of tents, and the camp was astir. Addie Knighton, still half-dazed with sleep, was led firmly by Gertrude Oliver to the edge of the lake and forced to wash her face.

"You'll thank me when you're really awake," purred Gertie, ignoring her victim's protests. "It's only what I promised you faithfully last night. You told me to duck you in, if nothing else would do it."

"Oh, I'm awake now! I am truly. You needn't be afraid I'll go back to bed," bleated Addie, afraid her friend might proceed to extremities. "Hadn't you better haul up Alice next?"

"I left Chrissie doing that. She's going round the tents with a wet sponge. Look! Isn't that worth getting up to see?"

The grey of the sky had flushed into carnation pink, and up

from behind the wall of the mountains rose the great ball of the sun, red at first through a veil of mist, but shining out golden as he cleared the cloud-bank. Everything was waking up. A peewit called by the water's edge, a cock crew from the farm-yard, and a dog barked lustily.

"Our thief of the night complaining of an attack of indigestion, I hope," said Ulyth, joining Addie and Gertie at the lake-side. "How much can a dog eat without feeling ill?"

"We had a collie that consumed three rabbits once," laughed Addie. "We didn't ask it how it felt afterwards. It got a good thrashing, I remember."

"We'll keep a stick handy to-night, in case of any more raids. Who's on breakfast duty? I'm getting wildly hungry. I hope the bacon hasn't disappeared with the mutton."

Although the three days' sojourn under canvas was in a sense a holiday, it was conducted in a very business-like spirit and with rigid discipline. All the daily duties were performed zealously by bands of servers, who polished tins, peeled potatoes, washed plates, or cleaned shoes, as the case might be. The League was putting to a practical proof the seven rules of the Camp-fire Law. Beauty was all around them, and knowledge to be had for the asking. They proved themselves trustworthy by their service, and glorified work in the doing of the camp tasks. Health was drawn with every breath of mountain air, and, judging from their faces, the seventh rule, "Be happy", seemed almost superfluous. Everyone looked radiant, even Mary Acton, who was a champion grumbler, and generally ready to complain of crumpled rose-leaves. After breakfast and service duty came drill, a more than usually formal affair, for Mr. Arnold himself reviewed them. He had great experience with the Boy Scouts, so the girls were anxious to do the utmost credit to their beloved

Guardian of the Fire. The Ambulance Corps gave a demonstration of First Aid; another detachment took down and re-erected a tent; the juniors showed their abilities in knot-tying, and the seniors in signalling. Their inspector declared himself perfectly satisfied, and commended certain members for special proficiency.

"I shall tell the boys' battalions how well you can do," he declared. "It will put them on their mettle. They won't want to be beaten by a ladies' school."

When the display was over, all dispersed for a ramble round the lake while the dinner stewed; only the cooks on duty remained, carefully watching their pots. Ulyth, Rona, Lizzie, and Gertrude wandered past the farm and up the hill-side to the head of a crag, whence they had a glorious view down over the sheet of water below.

"Llyn Gwynedd looks so cheerful and innocent now, one wouldn't believe it could ever be treacherous and do dreadful things," remarked Gertrude.

"What things?" asked Ulyth.

"Why, I believe someone was drowned just down there a great many years ago. I heard Catherine saying so last night, so I suppose it's true."

"It's perfectly true, and I can tell you who it was," answered Lizzie. "It was the eldest son of Lord Glyncraig. He was fishing here, and the boat got upset. It was the most dreadful tragedy. He was such a fine, promising young fellow, and had only been married quite a short time. He was the heir, too, which made it worse."

"But there are other sons, aren't there?" asked Ulyth.

"Yes, but he was the flower of the family. The rest are no good. The second son, the present heir, is a helpless invalid, the third is in a sanatorium for consumption, and the fourth was the proverbial prodigal, and disappeared. If Lord Glyncraig knows where he is, nobody else does."

"Hadn't the one who was drowned any children?"

"Only a girl. The second and third aren't married."

"Then will the estate have to go to the prodigal in the end?"

"I suppose so, if he's alive, and turns up to claim it."

"Peers have their troubles as much as commoners," commented Ulyth. "I've never heard this before. I'm sorry for Lord Glyncraig. Plas Cafn is too good to go to a prodigal."

"Yet prodigals sometimes turn out better than elder brothers, if we accept the parable," remarked Rona, throwing stones into the water as viciously as if she were aiming at an enemy.

"Don't!" said Ulyth. "You'll disturb the trout, and Mrs. Arnold wants to fish this afternoon. Rona, do stop! Let's go down to the edge again, and try and find some bog bean. You'll get a proficiency badge if you can show twenty specimens of wild flowers and name them. Yes, I won mine last year, and so did Lizzie."

"I'd rather win a proficiency badge for shooting," grunted Rona. "Why can't Teddie let us get up a ladies' rifle corps?"

"Only wish she would, just! It would be prime," agreed the others.

Dinner was ready by twelve o'clock—not at all too early for

a company that had breakfasted at seven. Despite the purloining of the leg of mutton there was enough to go round, and everybody decided that the cooks deserved proficiency badges. The servers also did their work promptly, and removed plates and dishes with the maximum of speed and the minimum of clatter. By half-past one everything was washed up and polished, and the kitchen department in apple-pie order.

"I'm afraid we may have rain," said Miss Teddington, looking anxiously at the sky, which was now completely overcast with clouds.

"One often gets a shower among the mountains when the valley escapes," commented Mrs. Arnold. "I don't think it will be much this afternoon, if there's rain at all. The patrols know what to do if it begins. This grey sky will be good for fishing."

Mrs. Arnold was an enthusiastic angler, and had brought her fishing-tackle with her to camp. She intended that afternoon to hire a boat from the farm and see if she could beguile some of the wily trout from the lake.

"I'll take four girls with me," she announced: "two to row, one to steer, and one to help with the landing-net."

Needless to say, she could have had dozens of volunteers, but her choice fell on Kathleen Simpson, Ruth White, Gladys Broughton, and Evie Isherwood, who, highly elated, went off to unmoor the boat. Then, Ruth and Kathleen rowing, and Gladys steering, they made gently down the lake towards the west end, where the stream flowed out.

Pretty Mrs. Arnold looked particularly charming in a blue-and-white boating-costume, with a little blue fisherman's cap perched on her fair hair. It was the fashion for the girls to adore her, and she certainly had four whole-hearted admirers with her that afternoon, ready to be at her beck and call, and to perform any service she wished. They followed her instructions to the letter, and watched her line and reel with tense eagerness.

"I hope we may catch some salmon trout," said Mrs. Arnold; "they're much more delicate than the ordinary ones. If we've luck we may get enough at any rate to give Miss Bowes and Miss Teddington a dish for supper. Row gently along there, I saw a fish jump; if it's hungry it may fancy my fly. Good biz! there's a bite. I'll have to play him gently; he feels a strong fellow. Are you ready, Evie, with the landing-net?"

It was frightfully exciting as Mrs. Arnold wound her reel, and the prey came within reach. Was he really hooked, or would he break away at the last moment and disappoint them?

"We've got him! We've got him! Quick, Evie! Oh, I say! Isn't he splendid?"

A silvery-grey, gleaming, glittering object was leaping in the landing-net at the bottom of the boat.

"Oh, what luck!" yelled Evie.

"He must be a patriarch!" cried the rowers.

"I can't see him. Oh, do let me look!" squealed Gladys, forgetting everything in her eagerness. "Ruth, you're in the way. I must look."

And up she sprang, trying to push past Ruth and Kathleen.

Angela Brazil

"Sit still!" shouted Mrs. Arnold frantically, but the mischief was done.

It all happened in two seconds. No one quite knew how, though Ruth declared afterwards that in trying to scramble past her Gladys stepped on the gunwale. Over toppled the boat, and almost before its occupants knew their danger they were struggling in the water. The girls could swim a little—a very little. Kathleen, gasping and spluttering, struggled valiantly towards the bank; Evie, with a certain instinct of self-preservation, turned on her back, and managed to keep herself afloat somehow. Ruth and Gladys clutched the upturned boat and, clung there screaming. Mrs. Arnold was in even more desperate straits. She could not swim, and she had fallen too wide of the boat to be able to grasp it. The few patrols left in charge of the camp stood for a moment paralysed, then tore along the side of the lake towards the scene of the accident. But someone else was quicker. Rona, hunting for botany specimens, had been watching the fishing from the bank close by. There was a rush, a splash, a swift little figure wildly ploughing a path through the lake, beating the water with short, impatient strokes.

"I won't clutch you," cried Mrs. Arnold, pluckily keeping her presence of mind. "I believe I can manage to float."

She lay still as Rona put a hand under her shoulder and towed her towards the shore, so still that she neither stirred nor spoke when Doris and Catherine, who had reached the spot, helped to drag her from the water.

"Oh, she's drowned!" shrieked Doris.

"No, no! Lay her down flat. She's opening her eyes."

Marion Harper and Madge Johnson, both tolerable swimmers,

were plunging to help Evie; Kathleen was already struggling ashore. "Wait till we can come for you!" shouted Rona to Ruth and Gladys; "don't let go the boat."

Evie was pulled ashore first, not much the worse. Rona had trouble with Gladys, who had waxed hysterical, but with Marion's help she landed her safely and went back for Ruth. By this time the danger-signal, blown lustily from several League whistles, brought all who were anywhere within reach rushing to the rendezvous. Mrs. Arnold, with wet golden hair clinging round her white face, leaned against Catherine's shoulder, while Doris rubbed her hands.

"I'm glad my husband's gone to Capel Garmon to-day. Please let me tell him myself," were her first words. "It was good little Rona who saved me," she added, smiling faintly at Miss Bowes, who was down on her knees beside her on the grass.

"I wish I'd done it. I wish I'd done it. Oh, how I envy you, Rona!" cried Ulyth, regarding her friend with wide shining eyes of admiration.

Miss Teddington, pale but very self-controlled, had taken command of the situation. Eight people were thoroughly wet through and bedraggled, and must be hurried to camp and dried, and given hot drinks as speedily as possible. The rescuers needed cosseting as much as the rescued. Madge and Marion were shivering and trembling, and Rona, now the excitement of her sudden dash was over, looked more shaky than she would allow.

"We must tuck them up in blankets," said Miss Teddington. "First Aid Corps on duty, please! The difficulty is going to be how to get their clothes properly dried in a place like this."

Mrs. Arnold, with Miss Bowes to look after her, went to the farm to seek fresh garments. As for the girls, there was nothing for it but to go to bed for an hour or two, while a band of servers lighted a good fire, wrung the water from the drenched articles of clothing, and held them to the blaze. Blankets were commandeered freely from other beds, and piled round the seven heroines, who, propped up with pillows, each had a kind of reception as she sipped her hot cocoa.

"We all of us forgot about the boat," said Rona suddenly. "It's drifting upside down, and the oars are anywhere."

"Never mind. David Lewis will get it somehow, I suppose. It will drift towards the bank, and he'll wade for it."

"Where did you learn to swim like that, Rona?"

"In the lake at home. We had one nearly as big as this close to our farm."

"The Cuckoo's turned up trumps," murmured Alice Denham. "I didn't know she was capable of it."

"Then it only shows how extremely stupid and unobservant you are," snapped Ulyth.

The servers declared afterwards that drying clothes round a bonfire was the most exciting duty they had ever performed. Gusts of wind blew the flames in sudden puffs, necessitating quick snatching away of garments in the danger zone. Shoes were the most difficult of all, and needed copious greasing to prevent their growing stiff.

"I wonder if the Ancient Britons went through this performance?" said Winnie Fowler. "Did they have to hold their skin garments round camp-fires? Thank goodness, we've got these things dry at last! We're only in the nick of time. Here comes the rain."

It was a melancholy truth. The Welsh mountains have a perverse habit of attracting clouds, even in June; the sky, which had been overcast since midday, was now inky dark, and great drops began to fall. It was a calamity, but one for which everybody was fully prepared. The patrols rushed round the camp loosening ropes, lest the swelling hump should draw the pegs from the ground, and took a last tour of inspection to see that no bed was in contact with the canvas.

"If you even touch the inside of the tent with your hand you'll bring the water through," urged Catherine in solemn warning; "so, for your own sakes, you'd best be careful. You don't want to spend the night in a puddle."

It was a new experience to sit inside tents while the storm howled outside. Rain up at Llyn Gwynedd was no mere summer shower, but a driving deluge. Servers in waterproofs scuttled round with cans of hot tea and baskets of bread and butter, and the girls had a picnic meal sitting on their beds. One tent blew over altogether, and its distressed occupants, crawling from under the flapping ruin, were received as refugees by their immediate neighbours. Fortunately the storm, though severe, was short. By seven o'clock it had expended its fury, and passed away down the valley towards Craigwen, leaving blue sky and the promise of a sunset behind. Glad to emerge from their cramped quarters, the girls came out and compared experiences. There was plenty to be done. The fallen tent had to be erected, and various cans and utensils which had been left outside must be collected and wiped before they had time to rust.

"This is the prose of camp-life," said Catherine, picking the

Angela Brazil

gravy-strainer out of a puddle and rinsing it in the lake. "I hope we shall get the poetry to-morrow again."

"Oh, it's lovely fun when it rains!" twittered some of the younger ones.

Mr. Arnold came down from the farm to inquire rather anxiously how the camp was faring after the storm, and particularly to have news of the girls who had been in the lake. He had left Mrs. Arnold in bed, still rather upset with the shock of the accident.

"I feel responsible for bringing you all here," he said to Miss Teddington. "I shan't be easy in my mind now till the whole crew's safe back at The Woodlands."

"We've taken no harm," Miss Teddington assured him. "The girls kept dry, and they're as jolly as possible; indeed, I think most of them thoroughly enjoyed the rain."

Llyn Gwynedd, after showing what it could do in the way of storms, provided fine weather for the next day. The ground soon dried, and camp-life continued in full swing. Mrs. Arnold, herself again after a night's rest, took the morning drill, and led a ramble up the slope of Glyder Garmon in the afternoon. She was the heart and soul of the "stunt" that evening.

The girls, at any rate, were sorry to say good-bye to the lake on Friday morning, whatever their elders might feel on the subject.

"I hope the Boy Scouts will have as ripping a time as we've had," was the general verdict when, having left the camp in perfect order, the procession set out to tramp down to Aberglyn.

"Barring total immersions in the lake, please," said Mr. Arnold, as he returned the parting salute.

"But that was an opportunity," urged Ulyth. "I wish it had come my way. Rona, Madge, and Marion will all get special bravery medals at next quarterly meeting. I've no luck!"

Angela Brazil

CHAPTER XIV

SUSANNAH MAUDE

The girls at The Woodlands, while they contributed to various charities, had one special and particular object of interest. For several years they had supported a little girl at an orphanage. She was called their orphan, and twice a year they received accounts of her progress. They sent her a Christmas present annually, and her neat little letter of thanks was handed round for everybody to read. Poor Susannah Maude was the daughter of very disreputable parents; she had been rescued from a travelling caravan at the age of ten, and the authorities at the Alexandra Home had done their best to obliterate her past life from her memory. When she reached school-leaving age the question of her future career loomed on the horizon. After considerable correspondence with the matron, Miss Bowes had at length decided to have the girl at The Woodlands, and try the experiment of training her as a kitchen-maid. So in February Susannah Maude had arrived, small and undersized, with a sharp little face and beady, black eyes, and a habit of sniffing as if she had a perpetual cold.

"Not a bit like the blue-eyed, flaxen-haired orphan of fiction," decided the girls, rather disappointed at the sight of their protegee.

Perhaps the cook was disappointed too. At any rate, many complaints of smashed dishes, imperfect wiping, and inadequate sweeping of corners reached Miss Bowes, who urged patience, harangued the culprit, and shook her head, half laughing and half sighing, over the domestic catastrophes. Though strictly confined to the kitchen regions, the orphan took the deepest interest in the young ladies of the school. Her keen eyes would peer out of windows, and her head bob round doors in continual efforts to gain some idea of their mode of life. A chance word from one of them wreathed her in smiles. She was a funny, odd little object with her short squat figure and round bullet head, and thin little legs appearing underneath her official white apron. Her official name was Susan, but every girl in the school called her Susannah Maude. At the instigation of Miss Bowes her patrons took the furthering of her education in hand, and each in turn bestowed half an hour a day in hearing her read history, geography, or some other suitable subject. A little bewildered among so many fresh teachers, the small maid nevertheless made what efforts she could, and read loud and lustily, even if she did not altogether digest the matter she was supposed to be studying.

"I believe she reads the words without taking in a scrap of the sense," laughed Ulyth, when her turn as instructress was over. "She was gazing at my dress, or my watch, or my handkerchief whenever she could spare an eye from her book. She thinks them of far more importance than Henry VIII."

"So she does," agreed Lizzie. "I tried to get her interested yesterday in the number of his wives—I thought the Bluebeard aspect of it might move her—but she only said: 'What does it matter when they're all dead?' I felt so blank that I couldn't say any more."

Nobody quite remembered whose idea it was that their

orphan should be invited to the Camp-fire meetings. Somebody in a soft-hearted moment suggested it, and Mrs. Arnold replied: "Oh yes, poor little soul! Bring her, by all means." So Susannah Maude had come, and once there she apparently regarded herself as a member of the League, and turned up on every available occasion. How much she understood of the proceedings or of the scope of the society nobody could fathom. She sat, during the meetings, bolt upright, with folded arms, as if she were in school, her bright, beady eyes fixed unblinkingly upon Mrs. Arnold, whom she seemed to regard as a species of priestess in charge of occult mysteries.

"Would I be struck dumb if I told what goes on here?" she asked Ulyth one day; and, although she was assured that no such act of vengeance on the part of Providence would overtake her, she nevertheless preserved a secrecy worthy of a Freemason, and would drop no hint in the kitchen as to the nature of the ceremonies she witnessed.

One or two points evidently made a great impression upon her. During the spring months Nature lore was very much to the fore, and the members qualified for candidateship to the various grades by exhibiting their knowledge of the ways and habits of birds. Notes of observations were read aloud at the meetings, particulars recorded of nests that had been built in the school grounds, with data as to the number of days in which eggs were hatched and the young ones fledged. It was an unwritten law at The Woodlands never to disturb the birds. The girls were not allowed to take any eggs from the nests, and were taught not to frighten a sitting bird or to interfere with the fledge-lings. After several years of such consideration The Woodlands had become a kind of bird sanctuary, where the little songsters appeared to know they were free from molestation. That the fruit in the garden suffered rather a heavy toll was true; but, as Miss Bowes remarked: "One can't have everything. We must remember how many insects they clear away, and not grudge them a few currants and gooseberries. They pay us by their lovely songs in the spring."

Ulyth was a great devotee of Nature study, and had the supreme satisfaction of being the first to discover that a pair of long-tailed tits were building in a gorse-bush down the paddock. She was immensely excited, for they were rather rare birds in that district, and generally nested much higher up on the hills. This was indeed the only instance on record of their having selected The Woodlands for their domestic operations. As she had made the discovery, it was her particular privilege to take the observations, and every day she would go very quietly and cautiously and seat herself near the spot to note the doings of the shy little architects. It was a subject of intense interest to watch the globular nest grow, and then to ascertain, when the parents were out of the way, that eggs had actually been laid in it. Ulyth was so afraid of disturbing the tits that she conducted her daily observations alone, fearing lest even Lizzie's presence might frighten them. "When there are two of us we can't help talking, and an unusual sound scares them worse than anything," she decided.

One morning she started for her daily expedition to the paddock. The little hen had been sitting long enough to make Ulyth think the eggs must surely be hatched, and that probably the parents were both already busy catering for their progeny. She crept noiselessly round the corner to the hollow where the bushes were situated. Then she gave a gasp and a cry of horror. On the ground, quite close to the nest, knelt Susannah Maude, busily occupied in smearing some sticky white substance over the lower boughs and shoots of the gorse-bushes. She looked round with a beaming face as Ulyth approached. Her beady eyes twinkled with self-congratulation.

Angela Brazil

"Susannah! What are you doing, you young imp of mischief?" exclaimed Ulyth in an agony.

"Catching your birds for you, Miss," responded the orphan, a thrill of pride in her voice. "It's bird-lime, this is, and it'll soon stick 'em, you'll see. I knows all about it, for my father was a bird-catcher, and I often went with him when I was a kid. I'd a job to get the lime, I can tell you, but Bobby Jones brought me some from Llangarmon."

She looked at Ulyth with a smile, as if waiting for the praise that she deemed due to her efforts. Utterly aghast, Ulyth stammered:

"But, Susannah Maude, we—we don't want the birds caught."

The orphan appeared puzzled. A shade crossed her sharp little face.

"Not want to catch 'em? What's the use of 'em, then? Dad caught 'em and sold 'em."

Ulyth had to keep a strong curb over her temper. After all, how could this ignorant child know what she had never been taught? Miss Bowes might well preach patience and forbearance.

"It's very cruel to snare the birds with lime at any time, especially now, when they have young ones who would starve without them," she explained with what calm she could muster. "Promise me that you will never try to do such a thing again, and never interfere with any of the nests. Mrs. Arnold will be most grieved to hear of this."

The orphan's black eyes filled with tears.

"Will she mind? I thought she'd like 'em to keep in a cage as pets. I'd do anything in the world to please her."

"Then leave the birds alone, if you want to please her. Run now to the house and fetch me a basin full of hot water and a cloth. I must wipe all this horrible stuff off the bushes. Bring a knife, too, for I shall have to cut away some of the branches and burn them. I hope the tits won't desert."

Ulyth was late for school that morning, but the offence was condoned by Miss Teddington when she heard the reason.

"I hope you washed every scrap of the lime off?" she asked anxiously.

"I didn't leave it while there was enough to catch even a bumble-bee. The birds are back. They came directly I'd gone a dozen yards away."

"That shows the young ones are hatched. I hope Susan won't direct her energies into any other natural-history experiments."

"We shall be sorry we brought her to the Camp-fire if she does. She means well, but the worst of her is that you never can calculate in the least what she may do next. She's a problem."

*   *   *   *   *

During the summer term the Camp-fire Guild had many informal meetings by the stream. The girls were often allowed to take tea there, a permission which they highly appreciated. Mrs. Arnold had lent them a small camp-oven, in which they could bake cakes, and many culinary efforts resulted from the acquisition. On Saturday afternoon

Gertrude Oliver and Addie Knighton were on the cooking-list as special scouts, and, having mixed some currant-buns, placed them carefully in the oven. They were in charge of the camp-fire and responsible for the preparation of the tea, to which that day all the mistresses were to be specially invited. The rest of the school were in the playing-field practising flag-signalling under the joint superintendence of Mrs. Arnold and Miss Teddington.

"It's a nuisance we can't leave the cakes," sighed Addie. "I did so want to see them send that message about the aeroplane."

"They're baking all right," said Gertrude. "We can't make them any quicker by looking at them. Couldn't we just run to the top of the gravel-pit and watch for a few minutes? There's Susannah Maude; she'd keep an eye on them. Hello! Susan!"

The orphan, in virtue of being a hanger-on of the Camp-fire, was wandering about by the stream in the wake of the proceedings. She came running up eagerly at Gertrude's call.

"I'll mind 'em for you, Miss. I've watched Cook dozens of times. I'll look after the kettle too. You leave it to me."

"I hope it won't be a case of King Alfred and the cakes."

Susan grinned comprehension.

"Standard V Historical Reader. Not me!" she chuckled. "I always thought the woman was a silly to trust a man to turn the cakes."

"Well, mind you show up better. You might as well put the milk-can in the stream to keep cool. We don't want it curdled, and I'm certain there's thunder about."

Addie and Gertie were sure they were not absent long. They just stood and watched a few messages being sent, then ran back promptly to their duties.

Susannah Maude was in the very act of trying to lift the big camp-kettle from its trivet.

"Hold hard there!" screamed Addie, running to the rescue. "You can't move that alone. Susan! Stop!" It was too late, however. The small busybody had managed to stir the kettle, but, her youthful arms being quite unequal to sustaining its weight, she let it drop, retreating with a wild Indian yell of alarm. The stream of boiling water fortunately escaped her, but nearly put out the fire. When the steam and dust had subsided, the rueful scouts picked up the empty kettle gingerly, as it was hot.

"We shall have to build up the fire again," lamented Gertrude. "Oh, Addie, the cakes!"

She might well exclaim. In a row among the ashes were the soaked, dust-covered remains of the precious currant-buns.

"I took 'em out of the oven because they were done," explained Susan hastily, justifying herself. "I thought you shouldn't blame me for letting 'em burn, anyhow; and I put 'em down there on some dock-leaves to keep hot. I couldn't tell the kettle would fall on 'em."

"They're done for," sighed Addie. "There isn't one fit to eat. Help us to fill the kettle again as soon as you can, and fetch some more sticks and gorse, you black-eyed Susan!"

"Where's the milk-can?" asked Gertrude uneasily.

Angela Brazil

"I put it in the stream as you told me," replied the orphan rather sulkily, indicating with a nod the location.

Decidedly anxious as to its safety, the girls ran to the waterside. They always put the can in a particular little sheltered corner fenced in by a few stones. Susannah had helped them to place it there many times, and had even named the spot "the dairy". They looked in vain. The milk was certainly not there now.

"What in the name of thunder have you done with the can, you wretched imp?" shouted Addie, thoroughly angry.

"You said it ought to keep very cool, so I threw it into the deep pool. 'Tain't my fault," retorted Susannah, who had a temper as well as her benefactresses.

"I've half a mind to throw you after it!" raged Gertie, her fingers twitching to shake the luckless orphan.

Perhaps Susannah's experienced eye gauged the extent of her wrath, and decided that for once she had gone too far. She did not wait to proffer any more explanations, but turned and fled back towards the house, resuming her neglected pan-scouring in the scullery with a zeal that astonished the cook.

Addie and Gertie replenished the camp-fire and refilled the kettle; but the cakes were hopeless, and the milk was beyond recall. Doris Deane, the champion swimmer of the school, dived for the can next morning and brought it up empty; the lid was never recovered, probably having been washed into a hole.

The Guild sat down that afternoon rather disconsolately to milkless tea. Addie had begged a small jugful from the kitchen, enough for their guests, the mistresses, but it was impossible to replace the big two-gallon can at a moment's notice.

"I begin to wish the school had never supported an orphan at the 'Alexandra Home for Destitute Children'," sighed Gertie, eating plain bread and butter, and thinking regretfully of her spoilt cakes. "I vote next term we ask to give up collecting for it, and keep a monkey at the Zoo instead. We could send it nuts and biscuits at Christmas."

"And currant-buns?" giggled Beth Broadway.

"You are about the most unfeeling wretch I ever came across!" snapped Gertrude.

CHAPTER XV

A POINT OF HONOUR

"Lizzie," announced Ulyth, sitting down on a stump in the glade, and speaking slowly and emphatically, "The Woodlands isn't what it used to be."

"So Stephanie was saying the other day," agreed Lizzie, taking a seat on the stump by the side of her friend. "She thinks it's a different place altogether."

"It is; though not exactly from Stephie's point of view. I don't care the least scrap that there are no Vernons or Courtenays or Derringtons here now. Stephie can lament them if she likes. I never knew them, so I can't regret them. There's one thing I can't help noticing, though—the tone has been going down."

"Do you think it has?" replied Lizzie thoughtfully. "Merle and Alice and Mary are rather silly, certainly, but there's not much harm in them."

"I don't mean our form; it's the juniors. I've noticed it continually lately."

"Now you come to speak of it, so have I. I don't quite know

what it is, but there's a something."

"There's a very decided something. It's come on quite lately, but it's there. They're not behaving nicely at all. They've slacked all round, and do nothing but snigger among themselves over jokes they won't tell."

"They're welcome to their own jokes as far as I'm concerned, the young idiots!"

"Yes, if it's only just fun; but I'm afraid it's something more than that—something they're ashamed of and really want to hide. I've seen such shuffling and queer business going on when any of the monitresses came in sight."

"Have you said anything to Catherine or Helen?"

"No, and I don't want to. It's very unfortunate, but they've really got no tact. Catherine's so high-handed, and Helen's nearly as bad. They snap the girls up for the least trifle. The result is the juniors have got it into their tiresome young heads that monitresses are a species of teacher. They weren't intended to be that at all. A monitress is just one of ourselves, only with authority that we all allow. She ought to be jolly with everybody."

"Um! You can hardly call Catherine jolly with the kids."

"That's just it. They resent it; they've gone their own way lately, and it's been decidedly downhill. I'm persuaded they're playing some deep and surreptitious game at present. I wish I knew what it was."

"Can't Rona tell you?"

"I wouldn't pump Rona for the world. It's most frightfully

Angela Brazil

difficult for her, a junior, to be room-mate with a senior. Her form always suspect her of giving them away to the Upper School. Rona's had a hard enough struggle to get any footing at all at The Woodlands, and I don't want to make it any harder for her. If she once gets the reputation of 'tell-tale' she's done for. Since Stephanie made that fuss about juniors coming into senior rooms I mayn't ask her into V B; so if she's ostracized by her own form too she'll be neither fish, flesh, fowl, nor good red herring. No; however I find out it mustn't be through Rona."

"Yes, I quite see your point. Now you speak of it, I believe those juniors are up to something. There's a prodigious amount of whispering and sniggering among them. 'What's the joke?' I said to Tootie Phillips yesterday, and she flared out in the most truculent manner: 'That's our own business, thank you!'"

"Tootie has been making herself most objectionable lately. She wants sitting upon."

"Catherine will do that, never fear."

"No doubt, but it doesn't bring us any nearer finding out what those juniors are after."

"They vanish mysteriously after tea sometimes. I vote we watch them, and next time it happens we'll stalk them."

"Right-O! But not a word to anybody else, or it might get about and put them on their guard."

"Trust me! I wouldn't even flicker an eyelid."

Now that Ulyth and Lizzie had compared notes on the subject of the juniors, they became more convinced than ever of the fact that something surreptitious was going on. Nods, hints, words which apparently bore a hidden meaning, nudges, and signs were the order of the day. All friendly advances on the part of seniors were repelled, the younger girls keeping strictly to themselves. This was the more marked as there had never been any very great division at The Woodlands between Upper and Lower School, the whole of the little community sharing in most of the general interests.

After tea there was a short interval before evening preparation began, and during the summer term this was spent, if possible, out-of-doors by everybody. One afternoon, only a few days after the conversation just recorded, the girls had filed as usual from the dining-hall, and were racing off for tennis, basket-ball, or a run by the stream. As Ulyth, down on her knees in the darkest part of the hall cupboard, groped for her mislaid tennis-shoes, two members of IV B came in for a moment to fetch balls. They were in a hurry and they evidently did not perceive her presence.

"Did you get the tip?" Irene Scott asked Ethel Jephson under her breath. "By the lower pool immediately."

"All serene! Tootie told me herself."

"Pass it on then; though I think most know."

As they ran down the passage, Ulyth, relinquishing her hunt for the missing shoes, rose to her feet.

"There's one here who didn't know," she chuckled. "This is a most important piece of information. Immediately, by the lower pool, is it? Well, I must go and find Lizzie. What are those precious juniors up to, I wonder?"

Lizzie was taking her racket for a game of tennis, but she

readily gave up her place to Merle Denham at a hint from Ulyth.

"I told you they vanished after tea," she said, as the two girls sauntered into the glen. "We'll track them this time. Don't on any account look as if you were going anywhere. Sit down here and give them a few minutes' grace, in case stragglers come up. They probably won't begin punctually. I'll time it by my watch."

When five minutes had elapsed there was not a solitary junior to be seen in the glade, and Ulyth and Lizzie, deeming themselves safe, set out in the direction of the lower pool.

This was a part of the stream at the very verge of the grounds belonging to The Woodlands; indeed, the greater portion of it lay in the land of a neighbouring farmer, and to reach its pebbly bank meant a scramble round some palings and under a projecting piece of rock.

Ulyth and Lizzie were too wary to follow the juniors by this path, but scaled the palings at another point, and under cover of a thick copse of gorse-bushes approached the pool from the side that lay in the farmer's field. By most careful scouting they found a spot on the bank where they could see and hear without being seen.

Below them, seated on the rocks by the edge of the water, were practically almost the whole of the Lower School. They cuddled close, with their arms round each other, and to judge from their repressed giggles they appeared to be enjoying themselves. Tootie Phillips, a long-legged, excitable girl of thirteen, mounted upon a boulder, was addressing them with much fervour. Ulyth and Lizzie missed the beginning of her remarks, but when they came within earshot they realized that she was in the midst of a vigorous harangue against the seniors.

"Are we to be trodden down just because we're a little younger than they are?" urged Tootie. "Why should they lord it over us, I should like to know? They were juniors themselves only a year or two ago. I tell you the worm will turn."

"It's turned pretty considerably," guffawed Cissie Newall.

"It knows which side its bread's buttered," cackled Irene Scott.

"Buttered! You mean sugared, don't you?"

At this sally the whole party broke into a shout of laughter.

"Good for you, Ciss!"

"Sugared! Ra—ther!"

"Shut up, you sillies! Someone will hear us," commanded Tootie. "I was saying before, we're not going to be sat upon, either by teachers or monitresses or seniors. We'll take our own way."

"A sugary way," chirped Ethel Jephson.

The girls hinnied again. There was evidently something underlying the joke.

"When perfectly ridiculous rules are made, that never ought to have been made," continued Tootie, "then we've a right to take the law into our own hands and do as we please."

"Our pocket money's our own," grumbled a discontented spirit from the back.

"Of course it is, and we ought to be able to do what we like

Angela Brazil

with it."

"And so are our brooches, if we want to—"

"Sh—sh!"

"Shut up, stupid!"

"Well, we all know."

"No need to blare it out, if we do."

"I wasn't blaring."

"Violet Robertson, remember your oath," commanded Tootie. "If you let a word of—we know what—leak out, you're sent to Coventry for the rest of the term. Yes. Not a single one of us will speak one single word to you. Not even your own room-mates. So there!"

"Well, you needn't make such a precious fuss. I'm sure I wasn't letting out secrets," retorted Violet sulkily. "But I think there ought to be some rate of value. My brooch was a far better one than Mollie's."

"Right you are, my hearty, and I'm going to speak about it. We mustn't let ourselves be done, even by—you know who!"

"And she's sharp."

"She's getting too sharp. We must stop it, even if we have to break off for a whole week."

"No, no!"

"Oh, not that anyhow!"

"Well, look here, if you're such sillies, you deserve—"

But at this most interesting point the loud clanging of the preparation-bell put a stop to any further argument. With one accord the girls jumped up, and fled back as fast as they could run in the direction of the school. Ulyth and Lizzie, at the risk of being late for evening call-over, gave the conspirators time to get well away before they ventured to follow.

"What's the meaning of all this?" queried Lizzie, as they scouted cautiously through the glade.

"I can't imagine. They're evidently doing something they oughtn't to, the young wretches! But they're keeping it very dark."

"We shall have to watch them."

"We must indeed," sighed Ulyth. "Lizzie, I loathe eaves-dropping and anything that savours of underhand work, but what are we to do? Something is going wrong among the juniors, and for the sake of the school we've got to put it right if we possibly can. It's no use asking them their sweet secret, for they wouldn't tell us; and I'm afraid setting the monitresses on the track would only make things worse. If we can find out what they're doing, then we shall know our ground. I'm a Torch-bearer and you're a Fire-maker, and we must appeal to them to keep their Camp-fire vows. But we can't do that till we've some idea of which rule they're breaking. How can we say to them: 'I strongly suspect you're not being trustworthy'? We've got to prove our words."

"Prove them we will. We'll dodge about till we catch them in the act," agreed Lizzie.

To both the girls it was uncongenial though necessary work. As seniors and League officers they felt they owed a duty to the school, but that it would be far wiser to appeal privately to the juniors' sense of honour, and win them back to straight paths of their own free will, than to carry the matter to head-quarters. For the present, patience and tact must be their watchwords.

Several days went by, and nothing particular occurred. Either the younger girls were on their guard or they had suspended their activities. On Friday evening, however, as Ulyth was coming along the passage from practising, she accidentally cannonaded into half a dozen members of IV B who were standing near the boot cupboard. She evidently surprised them, for one and all they hastily popped their hands into their pockets. It was promptly done, but not so quickly as to prevent Ulyth from seeing that they were eating something.

"It's all right," gasped Bertha Halliwell, with apparent unconcern, in reply to Ulyth's apologies. "You nearly upset me, but I'm not fractured."

"I wish you'd take care, though," grumbled Etta Jessop, surreptitiously wiping a decidedly sticky mouth; "no one likes being tumbled over."

Ulyth passed on thoughtfully. What had they all been munching, and where did they get it from? Private supplies of cakes and sweets were utterly forbidden at The Wood-lands. Their prohibition was one of the strictest rules of the school, to break which would be to incur a very severe penalty from Miss Teddington. Was this the explanation of Tootie's rather enigmatical remarks down by the stream?

"If that's their precious secret, and they're just being greedy, I'm too disgusted with them for words!" commented Lizzie, when informed of the discovery.

Saturday and Monday passed with quite exemplary behaviour on the part of the juniors. The keenest vigilance could discover nothing. But on Tuesday Lizzie came across another clue. She had been monitress for the afternoon in the drawing-class, and after the girls had left she stayed behind to put away various articles that had been used and to tidy the room.

As she worked along the desks where IV B had been sitting, collecting stray pencils and pieces of india-rubber, she noticed a book lying on the floor and picked it up. It was a French grammar, with "Etta Jessop" written on the fly-leaf and had evidently been accidentally dropped. She turned over the pages idly. In the middle was a scrap of paper torn from an exercise-book, and on this was scribbled: "Where will she be to-night?" while in a different hand, underneath, as if in answer to the question, were the words: "Side gate at 8. Pass, 'John Barleycorn'."

This was most important. It was the first, indeed the only definite, information they had to go upon. Lizzie replaced the slip of paper and laid the book on the floor just where she had found it. Etta would no doubt soon discover her loss, and come back to fetch it. In the meantime this very valuable piece of news must be communicated to Ulyth.

The chums talked the matter over earnestly.

"Something's happening at the side gate at eight o'clock, and they've got a password; that's clear," said Lizzie.

"Then I think it's our plain duty to go and investigate," returned Ulyth. "If the worst comes to the worst we could report ourselves, and tell Teddie why we went. She'd understand."

"I hope it won't need that," fluttered Lizzie nervously.

The girls were not allowed out of the house after preparation, so any excursions into the garden were distinctly against the rules.

Feeling very culpable at thus breaking the law of the school, Ulyth and Lizzie crept quietly from the cloak-room door soon after eight had struck. It was not yet dark, but the sun had sunk behind the hills, and the garden was in deep shadow. They passed the tennis-courts and the rose parterre, and ran down the steps into the herbarium. Just at the outskirts of the shrubbery a small figure was skulking among the bushes. At the sound of footsteps it gave a low, peculiar whistle, then advanced slightly from the shadow and stood at attention, as if in mute challenge of the new-comers. Irene Scott, for it was she, was evidently on sentry duty. No one with a knowledge of camp-life could mistake her attitude.

"We'll bluff it off," whispered Ulyth, and, taking Lizzie's arm, she marched quietly past, murmuring: "John Barleycorn".

The effect of the password was electrical. Irene looked immensely astonished. She had certainly not expected such knowledge on the part of seniors.

"Are you in it too? Oh, goody!" she gasped; then very softly she called: "All's well!" and, turning, dived back among the bushes.

Lizzie and Ulyth pushed on towards the side gate. It was open, and inside, under the shelter of a big laurel, stood a woman with a basket. She was a gipsy-looking person, with long ear-rings, and she wore a red-and-yellow handkerchief tied round her neck. As the girls approached she uncovered her basket with a knowing smile.

"I've brought plenty to-night, Missies," she said ingratiatingly. "Cheesecakes and vanilla sandwiches and coco-nut drops and cream wafers. What'll you please to have?"

"Are you selling them?" asked Ulyth in much amazement.

The woman glanced at her keenly.

"I've not seen you two before," she remarked. "Yes, dearie, I'm selling them. They're wholesome cakes, and won't do you any harm. Try these cream wafers."

"No, thanks! We don't want anything," stammered Lizzie.

"If you've spent all your money," persisted the hawker, "I'm always open to take a trinket instead. There's a young lady been here just now, and gave me this in place of a sixpence," showing a small brooch pinned into her bodice. "Of course such things aren't worth much to me, but I'd do it to oblige you."

At the sight of the little brooch Ulyth flushed hotly.

"We're not allowed to buy cakes and tarts," she replied. "I'm sure Miss Bowes doesn't know that you come here to sell things. It's not your fault, of course, but please don't come again. It's breaking the rules of the school."

The woman covered up her basket in an instant.

"All right, Missie, all right," she said suavely. "I don't want to press things on you. That's not my way. You won't catch me at this gate again, I promise you. Good night!" and, slipping out into the lane, she was gone directly.

Ulyth shut the door and bolted it.

"She mayn't come to this particular spot again," said Lizzie, "but she'll find some other meeting-place, the cunning old thing. I could see it in her eye. So this is their grand secret! What a remarkably honourable and creditable one!"

"It's worse than I thought," groaned Ulyth. "They must have been going on with this business for some time, Lizzie. Do you know, that brooch was Rona's. I recognized it at once. It's one she brought from New Zealand, with a Maori device on it."

"I thought better of Rona."

"So did I. She's improved so much I didn't think she'd slip back in this way."

"I believe Tootie Phillips is the ring-leader."

"There's no doubt of it. From all we've seen, the juniors have got a systematic traffic with this woman, and post scouts to keep watch while she's about. You heard Irene call: 'All's well!'"

"They'll be feasting in their bedroom to-night."

"Rona won't dare, surely. Lizzie, I shouldn't have thought much of it if they'd done it once just for a lark. We're all human, and juniors will be juniors. But when it gets systematic, and they begin to sell their brooches, that's a different matter."

"What are you going to do? Tackle the kids and tell them we've found out, and they've got to stop it?"

"Will they really stop it just at our bidding? Or will it only put them on their guard and make them carry the thing on with more caution?"

"Then give a hint to the monitresses?"

"I wonder if we ought. I wish Catherine and Helen were different."

"Well, what do you suggest?"

"There's only one other way. Mrs. Arnold is coming to The Woodlands on Friday afternoon. Suppose we wait, catch her alone, and tell her all about it. She's our 'Guardian of the Fire', and we ought to be able to ask her things when we're in difficulties. She doesn't belong to the school, so it isn't like telling a teacher or a monitress. We know we can trust her absolutely."

"Right-O! But it seems a long time to have to wait."

"It can't be helped," said Ulyth, as they hurried back through the garden.

She had decided, as she thought, for the best, though, as the result proved, she had chosen a most unfortunate course.

Angela Brazil

CHAPTER XVI

AMATEUR CONJURING

Ulyth went to her bedroom that evening in much agitation of mind. She was torn by conflicting impulses. At one moment she longed to tax Rona frankly with a breach of school rules, air the whole subject, and state her most emphatic opinion upon it. If Rona alone had been concerned in the matter she would have done so without hesitation, but the knowledge of the number of girls who were involved made her pause.

"I might do more harm than good," she reflected. "After the way Tootie has been inciting them to take sides against the seniors, they'd be up in arms at the least hint. It will be worse if they know they're discovered, and yet go on in an even more underhand fashion."

Ulyth's abstraction was so marked that her room-mate could not fail to notice it.

"What's the matter with you to-night?" she asked. "I've never seen you so glum before. Have you been getting into a row with Teddie?"

"I'm all right. One can't always be talking, I suppose," returned Ulyth rather huffily. "Some people go on like a perpetual gramophone."

"Meaning Corona Margarita Mitchell, I suppose? As you like, O Queen! I'll shut up if my babble offends the royal ears. There! Don't look so tragic. I don't want to make myself a nuisance. But all the same it's depressing to see you looking like a mixture of Hamlet and Ophelia and Iphigenia and—and—Don Quixote. Was he tragic too? I forget."

"Hardly," said Ulyth, smiling in spite of herself.

"Well, I get mixed up among history and literature, can't always remember which is real and which is make-up. It's a fact. I put down Portia as history in my exercise yesterday, and said the story of the Spanish Armada was told by Chaucer. Now you're laughing, and you look more like Ulyth Stanton. Sit down on this bed. There! Open your mouth and shut your eyes, and see what the king will send you!"

Rona was fumbling in her drawer as she spoke. She turned round, seized her friend boisterously and forced her on to the bed, then, holding a hand over her eyes, crammed a chocolate almond into her mouth.

"Rona! What are you doing?" protested Ulyth, shaking herself free. "Where did you get this chocolate?"

Rona pulled a face expressive of mingled secrecy, delight, and triumph.

"Rats!" she chuckled enigmatically. "Little girls shouldn't ask questions."

"But I want to know."

"That's not sporty! Take the goods the gods send you, and

Angela Brazil

don't ask 'em what tree they picked them from."

"But, Rona—"

"Are you two girls still out of bed and talking?" said an indignant voice, as Miss Lodge opened the door and glared reproval. "Make haste. I give you three minutes, and if you're not ready by then I shall report you. Not another word! I'm astonished at you, Ulyth, for breaking the silence rule."

"I didn't hear the half-past nine bell," replied Ulyth, abashed.

"Then it's your business to hear it. It's loud enough. Everybody else on the landing is in bed."

Miss Lodge put out the light and walked away, with a final warning against further conversation. Rona was asleep in a few minutes, breathing calmly and peacefully as was her wont, but Ulyth lay awake for a long time watching a shadow on the wall cast from the beech-tree outside. Where had Rona got her chocolates? The answer was perfectly plain. With the little brooch for evidence there could be no mistake.

"She's not so bad as the others, because I really don't think she quite realizes even yet what school honour means. But Tootie and her scouts know. There's no excuse for them. Well, only two days now, and Mrs. Arnold will be here. What a tower of strength she is! I can tell her everything. Friday will very soon come now, thank goodness!"

But those two days were to bring events of their own, events quite unprecedented in the school, and unexpected by everybody. How they affected Ulyth and Rona will be related farther on in our story; but meantime, for a true understanding of their significance, we must pause to consider a certain feature of the life at The Woodlands. When Miss Teddington had joined partnership with Miss Bowes she had added many new ideas to the plan of education which had formerly been pursued.

She was determined that the school should not be dubbed "old-fashioned", and by all means in her power she kept it abreast of the times. So well did she succeed that the girls were apt to complain that their second Principal was a crank on education, and fond of trying every fresh experiment she could get hold of. The various enterprises added an atmosphere of novelty, however, and prevented the daily life from degenerating into a dull routine. No one ever knew what scheme Miss Teddington might suggest next; and even if each course was not pursued for very long, it did its work at the time, and was a factor in the general plan. All kinds and varieties of health exercises had had their day at The Woodlands—poles, dumb-bells, clubs, had been in turn discarded for deep breathing or for swimming motions. Slow minuets or lively tarantellas were danced, according to the fashion of the moment, and had the virtue of teaching stately dignity as well as poetry of motion. It was rumoured sometimes that Miss Teddington, with her eye on the past, contemplated a revival of backboards, stocks, and chest-expanders; but those instruments of torture, fortunately, never made their appearance, much to the relief of the intended victims, who had viewed their advent with apprehension.

Naturally, dancing and indoor P.T. went on mostly in the winter months, their place being taken by outdoor drill during the summer term. The Camp-fire movement had appealed to Miss Teddington. She would herself have liked to be "Guardian of the Fire" and general organizer of the League, but her better judgment told her it was wiser to leave that office to one who had not also to wield the authority of a teacher. She supported the League in every way that came within her province. As Camp-fire honours were given for nature study, astronomy, and geology, she took care that all had a chance to qualify in those directions; and lately, acting on a hint from Mrs. Arnold, she had made a special point of manual training. Since Christmas the studio had assumed a new importance in the school. It was a big glass-roofed room at the top of the house, reached by a small stair from the west bedroom landing. A carpenter's bench stood at one end of it, and wood-carving went on fairly briskly. The girls might come in at any time during their recreation hours, and the occupation was a great resource on wet days. Bookbinding, stencilling, clay modelling, and fretwork were included among the hobbies, and though there might not be definite lessons given, there were handy primers of instruction on the book-shelf, and it was interesting to try experiments.

"Do something on your own initiative. Take the book and puzzle it out, even if you make a few mistakes," urged Miss Teddington. "Nothing but practice can give you the right feel of your tools; you'll learn more from a couple of failures than from a week's work with a teacher at your elbow the whole time, saying 'Don't!'"

So the girls struggled on, making merry at each other's often rather indifferent efforts, but gaining more skill as they learnt to handle the materials with which they worked. If the mallet hit the chisel so vigorously as to spoil a part of the pattern, its wielder was wiser next time; and the experimenters in pyrography soon learned that a red-hot needle used indiscreetly can dig holes in leather instead of ornamenting it. Such "dufferisms", as the girls called them, became rarer, and many quite creditable objects were turned out, and judged worthy of a temporary place on the view-shelf.

Since Christmas a very special feature had been added to the handicraft department. Miss Teddington had caused apparatus to be fixed for the working of art jewellery. A furnace and a high bench with all necessary equipment had been duly installed. This was a branch much too technically difficult for the girls to attempt alone, so a skilled teacher had been procured, who came weekly from Elwyn Bay to give lessons. Those girls who took the course became intensely enthusiastic over it. To make even a simple chain was interesting, but when they advanced to setting polished pebbles or imitation stones as brooches or pendants, the work waxed fascinating. Some of the students proved much more adept than others, and turned out really pretty things.

There was not apparatus for many pupils to work, so the class had been limited to seniors, among whom Doris Deane, Ruth White, and Stephanie Radford had begun to distinguish themselves. Each had made a small pendant, and while the craftsmanship might be amateurish, the general effect was artistic. Miss Teddington was delighted, and wishing to air her latest hobby, she decided to send the three pendants, together with some other specimens of school handiwork, to a small Art exhibition which was to be held shortly at Elwyn Bay. Miss Edwards, the teacher who came weekly to give instruction, was on the exhibition committee, and promised to devote a certain case to the articles, and place them in a good light. Though small shows had been held at The Woodlands occasionally in connection with the annual prize distribution, the school had never before ventured to send a contribution to a public exhibition, and those whose work was to be thus honoured became heroines of the moment.

On the very evening after Ulyth's and Lizzie's excursion down the garden, a number of girls repaired to the studio to view the objects that Miss Teddington had chosen as worthy to represent the artistic side of the school.

"I wish I were a senior," said Winnie Fowler plaintively. "I'd have loved this sort of thing. To think of being able to make a little darling, ducky brooch! It beats drawing hollow. I'd never want to touch a pencil again."

"You've got to have some eye for drawing, though," said Doris, "or you'd have your things all crooked. It's not as easy as eating chocolates, I can tell you!"

"I dare say. But I'll try some day, when I am a senior."

"Are these the three that are to go to the exhibition?" asked Rona, pushing her way to the front. "Which is which?"

"This is mine, that's Ruth's, and that's Stephanie's," explained Doris.

"Why isn't Ulyth's to go? It's just as nice as Stephanie's, I'm sure."

"Miss Teddington decided that."

"How idiotic of her! Why couldn't she send Ulyth's? I think hers is the nicest, and it's just the same pattern as Stephie's—exactly."

"Do be quiet, Rona!" urged Ulyth, laying her hand on the arm of her too partial friend. "My pendant has a defect in it. I bungled, and couldn't get it right again afterwards."

"It doesn't show."

"Not to you, perhaps; but any judge of such things would notice in a moment."

"Well, your work's as good as Stephanie's any day, and I hate for her name to be put into the catalogue and not yours. Yes,

I mean what I say."

"Oh, Rona, do hush! I don't want my name in a catalogue. Here's Stephie coming in. Don't let her hear you."

"I don't mind if she does. It won't do her any harm to hear somebody's frank opinion."

"Rona, if you care one atom for me, stop!"

Rather grumbling, Rona allowed herself to be suppressed. She was always ready to throw a shaft at Stephanie, though she knew Ulyth heartily disliked the scenes which invariably followed. She took up Ulyth's pendant, however, and, after ostentatiously admiring it, laid it for a moment side by side with Stephanie's.

"There isn't a pin to choose between them," she murmured under her breath, hoping Stephanie might overhear.

Ulyth was at the other side of the room, but Stephanie's quick ears caught the whisper. She looked daggers at Rona, but she made no remark, and Ulyth, returning, gently took her pendant away and placed it with the other non-exhibits on the bench. It had been a wet afternoon. No outdoor exercise had been possible that day, and the girls were tired of all their usual indoor occupations.

"I wish somebody'd suggest something new to cheer us up," yawned Nellie Barlow. "There's a quarter of an hour more 'rec.' It's too short to be worth while getting out any apparatus, but it's long enough to be deadly dull."

"Can't someone do some tricks?" asked Edie Maycock.

"All right, Toby; sit on your hind legs and beg for biscuits," laughed Marjorie Earnshaw.

"I mean real tricks—conjuring and fortune telling; the amateur wizard, you know."

"I don't know."

"Then you're stupid. Have you never seen amateur conjuring—coins that vanish, and things that come out of hats?"

"Yes; but I couldn't do it, my good child. Being in the Sixth doesn't make me a magician."

"We tried a little bit at home," pursued Edie. "We had a book that told us how; only I never could manage it quickly. People always saw how I did it."

"Rona's the girl for that," suggested Hattie Goodwin.

"Is she? Come here, Rona, I want you. Can you really and truly do conjuring?"

"Oh, not properly!" laughed Rona. "But when I was on board ship there was a gentleman who was very clever at it, and I and some boys I'd made friends with were tremendously keen at learning. We got him to show us a few easy tricks, and we were always trying them. I could manage it just a little, but I'm out of practice now. You'd see in a second how it was done, I'm afraid."

"Oh, do show us, just for fun!"

"What do you want to see?"

"Oh, anything!"

"The vanishing coin?"

"Yes, yes. Go ahead!"

"Then give me two pennies or shillings, either will do."

The audience who had clustered round looked at one another, each expecting somebody else to produce a coin. Then everybody laughed.

"We haven't got so much as a copper amongst us! We're a set of absolute paupers!" declared Doris. "Can't you do some other trick?"

"There is nothing else I could manage so well," said Rona disconsolately. "This was the only one I really learnt."

"Can't it be done with anything but coins?"

"Something the same size and round, perhaps?"

"My pendant?" said Ulyth, fetching the trinket from the bench. "It's just as big as a penny."

"Yes, I could try it with this and another like it. Give me Stephanie's."

"No, no! You shan't try tricks with mine!" objected Stephanie indignantly.

"I won't do it a scrap of harm."

"Oh, Stephie, don't be mean! She'll not hurt it. Here, Rona, take it!" exclaimed several of the girls, anxious to witness the experiment.

Stephanie's protests and grumbles were overridden by the majority, and Rona, in her new capacity of wizard, faced her audience.

"It'll be rather transparent, because you oughtn't really to know that I've got two pendants," she explained apologetically. "Please forget, and think it's only one. I must put some patter in, like Mr. Thompson always used to do. Ladies and gentleman, you've no doubt heard that the art of conjuring depends upon the quickness of the hand. That's as it may be, but there is a great deal that can't be accounted for in that way. Ladies and gentlemen, you see this coin—or rather pendant, as I should say. I am going to make it fly from my left hand to my right. One, two, three—pass! Here it is. Did you see it go? No. Well, I can make it travel pretty quickly. Now we'll try another pretty little experiment. You see my hand. It's empty, isn't it? Yet when I wave it over this desk Miss Stephanie Radford's pendant will be returned to its place. Hey, presto! Pass! There you are! Safe and sound and back again!"

Stephanie took up her treasure and examined it anxiously.

"This isn't mine!" she declared.

"Rubbish! It is."

"I tell, you it isn't! Don't I know my own work? This is Ulyth's. What have you done with mine?"

"Vanished under the wizard's wand," mocked Rona.

"Give it me this instant!" cried Stephanie angrily, shaking Rona by the arm.

Rona had been standing upon one leg, and the unexpected

assault completely upset her balance. She toppled, clutched at Doris, and fell, bumping her head against the corner of the table. It was a hard blow, and as she got up she staggered.

"I feel—all dizzy!" she gasped.

An officious junior, quite unnecessarily, ran for Miss Lodge, magnifying the accident so much in her highly coloured account that the mistress arrived on the scene prepared to find Rona stretched unconscious. Seeing that the girl looked white and tearful, she ordered her promptly to bed.

"It may be nothing, but any rate you will be better lying down," she decreed. "Go downstairs, girls, all of you. Nobody is to come into the studio again to-night."

"Rona had my pendant in her hand all the time," grumbled Stephanie to Beth as she obeyed the mistress's orders. "She dropped it as she fell. I've put it back safely, though, and I don't mean to let anybody interfere with it. I shall complain to Miss Bowes if it's touched again."

CHAPTER XVII

A STORM-CLOUD

Rona woke up next morning without even a headache, in Miss Lodge's opinion "justifying the prompt measures taken", but according to the girls, "showing there had been nothing the matter with her to make such a fuss about". Breakfast proceeded as usual, and afterwards came the short interval before nine-o'clock school. Now on this day the contributions to the Art exhibition were to be packed up and dispatched by a special carrier, and Stephanie, as a budding metalworker, ran upstairs to the studio to take one last peep at her exhibit. She flew down again with white face and burning eyes.

"Girls!" she cried shakily. "Girls! Somebody's taken my pendant! It's gone!"

"Why, nonsense, Stephie; it can't be gone! It was there all right last night."

"It's not there now. Ulyth's has been put in its place, and mine's vanished. Come and see."

There was an instant stampede for the studio.

"It's probably on the bench," said Doris. "Some people are such bad lookers. I expect we shall find it directly."

"You can't find a thing that isn't there," retorted Stephanie with warmth.

Doris considered herself an excellent looker, and, in company with a dozen others, she searched the studio. Willing hands turned everything over, hunted under tables, on shelves, and among shavings, but not a sign of the pendant could they find.

"Are you sure this one isn't yours?" asked Ruth, coming back to the exhibits.

"Certain! I know my own work. This is Ulyth's; and there's the mistake she made that disqualified it."

"Yours was put back last night?"

"I saw it safe myself, after Rona'd been juggling with it. Where is Rona? I believe she's at the bottom of this."

"She's in the garden."

"Then she must be fetched."

"What's the matter? What are you making a bother about?" cried Rona, as an excited detachment of girls stopped her game of tennis and asked her a dozen questions at once. "What have I done with Stephanie's pendant? Why, I've done nothing with it, of course."

"But you must have hidden it somewhere."

"It's a mean trick to play on her."

"You and Steph are always at daggers drawn."

"Do go and put it back."

"I can't think what you're talking about!" flared Rona. "I've not even been inside the studio. If a joke's being played on Stephanie, it's somebody else who's doing it, not me. For goodness' sake let me get on with my game. Come, Winnie, it's your serve."

The girls retired, whispering to one another. They were not at all satisfied. The news of the loss spread rapidly over the school, and had soon reached the ears of the authorities. Miss Lodge, who heard it from a monitress, at once sought Miss Bowes' study. A few moments later she went in a hurry to summon Miss Teddington, and a rash junior who ventured within earshot was sent away with a scolding. Miss Bowes looked grave as she walked into the hall for call-over. She took the names as usual, then, instead of dismissing the forms, she paused impressively.

"I have something to say to you, girls," she began in a strained voice. "A most unpleasant thing has happened this morning. The pendant made by Stephanie Radford, which was to have been sent to the Elwyn Bay Exhibition, has disappeared, and Ulyth Stanton's pendant has been substituted for it. It is, I suppose, a practical joke on the part of one of you. Now I highly disapprove of this foolish form of jesting; it is neither clever nor funny, and is often very unkind. I beg whoever has done this thing to come forward at once and replace the pendant. She need have no fear, for she will not be punished or even scolded, though she must give me her word never to repeat such a prank."

Miss Bowes stopped, and looked expectantly at the rows of intent eyes fixed upon her. Nobody spoke and nobody moved. There was dead silence in the hall. The Principal flushed with annoyance.

"Girls, must I appeal to your honour? Is that necessary at The Woodlands? Have I actually one among you so lacking in moral courage that she dare not own up? I repeat that she will meet with no reproof. Nothing more will be said about the matter."

Still no reply. Each girl looked at her neighbour, but not even a whisper was to be heard.

"Girls, I am exceedingly pained. Such a thing has never happened here before. For the sake of the school, I make one last appeal to you. Will nobody speak? Then I shall be obliged to ask each of you in turn what she knows."

It was a dreary business putting the same question to forty-eight girls, receiving one after another forty-eight decided negatives. Miss Bowes sighed wearily as it came to an end, and turned to Miss Teddington, who had sat on the platform silent but frowning during the ordeal.

"We cannot let it rest here."

"Certainly not!" snapped Miss Teddington firmly. "The matter must be sifted to the bottom."

The two Principals conferred for a moment in whispers, then Miss Bowes announced:

"Girls, this affair must be very carefully inquired into. I hoped it was only a practical joke, but a circumstance came to my knowledge last night which, I fear, may lend a more sinister aspect to it than either Miss Teddington or I had imagined. I am most deeply disappointed that the code of honour which we have always upheld at The Woodlands seems by some of you to have been broken. I shall have more to say to you later on. In the meantime you may go to your classrooms."

Very solemnly the girls turned to march in their separate forms from the hall; but as IV B filed through the door there was a sudden outcry, a hustling, a rush of other girls, and an excited, aghast crowd.

"It's here! It's here, Miss Bowes!" shouted Doris Deane. "Rona Mitchell had it! It fell from her blouse pocket when she pulled out her handkerchief."

"It's Rona!"

"We saw it fall!"

"She had it all the time!"

"Oh, the sneak!"

"Silence!" thundered Miss Bowes, ringing her bell.

In the midst of the sudden hush the Principal walked down the hall and took the pendant from Doris's hand.

"What have you to say for yourself, Rona Mitchell?"

Rona was standing staring as if a ghost had suddenly risen up and confronted her. Her vermilion colour had faded, and left her face deadly white.

"Rona, do you hear me?"

Rona shivered slightly, glanced desperately at Miss Bowes,

then cast her eyes on the floor. She did not attempt to reply.

"I give you one more chance, Rona."

"Oh, Rona," interrupted Ulyth, who was weeping hot tears of dismay, "remember the Camp-fire! For the sake of the school, Rona!"

She drew back, choking with emotion, as Miss Bowes waved her aside.

Rona gazed for a moment full at Ulyth—a long, long, searching gaze, as if she would read Ulyth's very soul in her eyes. Then the colour flooded back, a full tide of crimson, over brow and neck.

"Yes—for the sake of the school!" she repeated unsteadily, and, bursting into tears, hid her burning face in her hands.

Miss Teddington hastily dismissed the other girls, and, coming to the assistance of her partner, asked many questions. It was absolutely useless, for Rona would not answer a single word.

"Go to your bedroom," said the irate Principal at last. "This matter cannot be allowed to pass. If you had owned up at once nothing would have been said, but such duplicity and obstinacy are unpardonable. Until you make a full confession you must not mix with the rest of the school. We should be sorry to have to send you back to New Zealand, but girls with no sense of honour cannot remain at The Woodlands."

Still sobbing hysterically, Rona was policed upstairs by Miss Teddington and locked into her bedroom. An hour or two of solitude might bring her to her senses, thought the mistress, and break the stubborn spirit which seemed at present to

Angela Brazil

possess her. A wide experience of girls had proved that solitary confinement soon quelled insubordination, and by dinner-time the culprit would probably volunteer some explanation.

Both Principals were greatly upset by the occurrence. Hitherto the little world at The Woodlands had jogged on without any more desperate happenings than the breaking of silence rules or the omission of practising. Never in all its annals had they been obliged to deal with a case of such serious import.

Ulyth, with the rest of V B, was obliged to march off to her form-room. The inquiry had delayed the morning's work, and Miss Harding began to give out books without a moment's further waste of time. Ulyth sat staring at the problem set her, without in the least taking in its details. She could not apply her mind to the calculation of cubic contents while Rona was crying her heart out upstairs. What did it, what could it, all mean? Had her room-mate only been intending to play a practical joke on Stephanie? If so, why had she not at once admitted the fact? Nobody would have thought much the worse of her for it, as such jokes had been rather the rage of late among the juniors. It seemed so unlike Rona to conceal it; lack of candour had not been her fault hitherto. She was generally proud of the silly tricks she was fond of playing, and anxious to boast about them. She could not have been deterred by dread of the Principals' displeasure. Only yesterday she had marched into the study, to report herself for talking, with a sangfroid that was the admiration of her form; and had come out again smiling, with the comment that both the Rainbow and Teddie were "as decent as anything if one owned up straight". No, there must be another and a much graver explanation.

A chain of circumstances flashed through Ulyth's mind, each

unfortunate link fitting only too well. The evidence seemed almost overwhelming. Rona had been present at the meeting by the stream when Tootie incited the juniors to some secret act of rebellion against the school rules. What this act was the occurrence in the garden had plainly shown. That Rona had been implicated seemed a matter of certainty. Her brooch had been in the possession of the cake-vendor, and she had chocolates in her bedroom, the acquisition of which she had refused to explain. Did she intend to keep the pendant and exchange it for confectionery? Her pocket-money, as Ulyth knew, was exhausted, and she had hardly any of the trinkets that most girls wear.

"Ulyth Stanton, you are not attending to your work. Give me your answer to Problem 46."

Ulyth started guiltily. Her page was still a blank, and she had no answer to produce. She murmured a lame excuse, and Miss Harding glared at her witheringly. Thrusting her preoccupation resolutely aside, she made an effort to concentrate her thoughts upon the subject in hand.

The morning passed slowly on. To Ulyth each successive class seemed interminable. At recreation, the girls, in small clumps, discussed the one topic of the hour.

"I'm not surprised. I'd think anything of Rona Mitchell," said Stephanie. "What else could you expect of a girl from the backwoods?"

"But she was so much improved," urged Addie, who had rather a weakness for the Cuckoo.

"Only a veneer. She relapsed directly she got the chance, you see."

Angela Brazil

"But why should she take your pendant?"

"I can't pretend to explain her motive, but take it she did—stealing, I should call it. But we're too polite at The Woodlands to use such a strong word."

"What'll be done to her?"

"Pack her back to New Zealand, I hope—and a good riddance. I always said she wasn't a suitable girl to come to this school. She hasn't the traditions of a lady. You might as well try to make a silk purse out of a sow's ear as to get such a girl to realize the meaning of *noblesse oblige*. It's birth that counts, after all, when it comes to the test."

"There I think you're wrong, Stephie," put in Lizzie quietly. "Gentle birth is all very well if it involves preserving a code of honour, but in itself it's no hall-mark of character. Some of the humblest and poorest people have been the stanchest on a question of right, when those above them in station have failed utterly. A charwoman can have quite as high standards as a duchess, and often lives up to them much better."

"Oh, you're a Radical!"

"I want fair play all round, and I must say that Rona has been very straight and square so far. Nobody has ever accused her of sneaking."

"No; the bear cub was unpolished, but not a vicious little beastie," agreed Addie.

"And it had grown wonderfully tame of late," added Christine.

Rona did not appear at the dinner-table; she had been

removed from her own bedroom to a small spare room on another landing. She still refused to answer any question put to her. Her silence seemed unaccountable, and the Principals could only consider it as a display of temper.

"She was annoyed at being caught red-handed with the pendant in her possession, and she won't give in and acknowledge her wrongdoing," said Miss Teddington to Miss Bowes.

"From a strong hint Cook gave me last night I fear there is something more behind it all," returned her partner. "I shall question every girl in the school separately until I get at the truth."

Beginning with the monitresses, Miss Bowes summoned each pupil in turn to her study and subjected her to a very strict catechism. From the Sixth she gained no information. They formed a clique amongst themselves, and knew little of the doings of the younger girls. V A were likewise absorbed in their own interests, and only classed Rona as one among many juniors. It was now the turn of V B, and Miss Bowes sent for Ulyth a trifle more hopefully. She, at least, would have an intimate knowledge of her room-mate.

"Have you ever known Rona mixed up in any deceit before? What is her general report among her form-mates?" asked the Principal.

"Very square. She used to annoy me dreadfully when first she came by turning over all my things, but she soon stopped when I told her how horrid it was. She never dreamt of taking anything. It was the merest curiosity; she hadn't been taught differently at home."

"Have you found her eating sweets or cakes in her bedroom lately?"

Ulyth hesitated and blushed.

"Ah! I see you have! You must tell me, Ulyth. Keep nothing back."

Very unwilling to betray her friend, Ulyth admitted the fact that chocolate had been pressed upon her one evening.

"Did Rona explain where she got it?"

"No, she wouldn't tell me anything."

Miss Bowes looked thoughtful.

"I put you upon your honour, Ulyth, to answer this question perfectly frankly. Have you any reason to suspect that some of the juniors have surreptitiously been buying cakes and sweets?"

Thus asked point-blank, Ulyth was obliged to relate what she had overheard; and Miss Bowes, determined to get at the root of the business, cross-questioned her closely, until she had dragged from her reluctant pupil the account of the occurrence in the garden and the conversation with the travelling hawker-woman.

"This is more serious even than I had feared," groaned Miss Bowes. "I thought I could have trusted my girls."

"I think most of them were ashamed of it," ventured Ulyth.

"It is just possible that Rona refuses to speak because she will not involve her schoolfellows."

"Oh yes, yes!" cried Ulyth, clutching at any straw to excuse her room-mate's conduct. "That's quite likely. Or, Miss

Bowes, I've been thinking that perhaps it was a queer kind of loyalty to me. You know Rona's very fond of me, and she was quite absurdly angry because Stephanie's pendant was to go to the exhibition and not mine. She may have changed them, hoping it wouldn't be noticed and that mine would be packed up, and perhaps she intended to put Stephanie's back in the studio when the parcel had safely gone. Rona does such impulsive things."

Miss Bowes shook her head sadly.

"I wish I could think so. Unfortunately the other circumstances lend suspicion to a graver motive."

CHAPTER XVIII

LIGHT

Ulyth walked from the study feeling that she had told far more than she wished.

"I've given Rona away," she said to herself. "Miss Bowes is thinking the very worst of her, I know. Oh dear! I wish she'd explain, and not keep up this dreadful silence. It's so unlike her. She's generally almost too ready to talk. If I could see her even for a few minutes I believe she would tell me. Perhaps Miss Teddington frightened her. Poor Rona! She must be so utterly miserable. Could I possibly get a word with her, I wonder?"

She talked the matter over with Lizzie.

"If I ask Miss Bowes, she'll probably say no," lamented Ulyth.

"Then I shouldn't ask," returned Lizzie. "We've not been definitely forbidden to see Rona."

"The door's locked."

"You've only to climb out of the linen-room window on to

the roof of the veranda."

"Why, so I could. Oh, I must speak to her!"

"I think you are justified, if you can get anything out of her. She'd tell you better than anybody else in the whole school."

"I'll try my luck then."

"I'll stand in the garden below and shout 'Cave!' if I hear anyone coming."

To help her unfortunate room-mate seemed the first consideration to Ulyth, and she thought the end certainly justified the means. She waited until after the tea interval, when most of the girls would be playing tennis or walking in the glade; then, making sure that Lizzie was watching in the garden below, she stole upstairs to the linen-room. It was quite easy to drop from the window on to the top of the veranda, and not very difficult, in spite of the slope, to walk along to the end of the roof. Here an angle of the old part of the house jutted out, and the open window of Rona's prison faced her only a couple of yards away. She could not reach across the gap, but conversation would be perfectly possible.

"Rona!" she called cautiously. "Rona!"

There was a movement inside the room, and a face appeared at the window. Rona's eyes were red and swollen with crying, and her hair hung in wild disorder. At the sight of Ulyth she started, and stared rather defiantly.

"Rona! Rona, dear! I've been longing to see you. I felt I must speak to you."

No reply. Rona, in fact, turned her back.

"I'm so dreadfully sorry," continued Ulyth. "I've been thinking about you all day. It's no use keeping this up. Do confess and have done with it."

Rona twisted round suddenly and faced Ulyth.

"Rona! You'd be so much happier if you'd own up you'd taken it. Surely you only meant it as a joke on Stephie? Miss Bowes will forgive you. For the sake of the school, do!"

Then Rona spoke.

"You ask me to confess—you, of all people!" she exclaimed with unconcealed bitterness.

"Yes, dear. I can't urge it too strongly."

"You want me to tell Miss Bowes that I took that pendant?"

"There's no sense in concealing it, Rona."

The Cuckoo's eyes blazed. Her hands gripped the window-sill.

"Oh, this is too much! It's the limit! I couldn't have believed it possible! You, Ulyth! you to ask me this! How can you? How dare you?"

Ulyth gazed at her in perplexity. She could not understand such an outburst.

"Surely I, your own chum, have the best right to speak to you for your own good?"

"My own good!" repeated Rona witheringly. "Yours, you mean. Oh yes, it's all very fine for you, no doubt! You're to get off scot free."

"I? What are you talking about?"

"Don't pretend you don't understand. You atrocious sneak and hypocrite—you took the pendant yourself!"

If she had been accused of purloining the Crown jewels from the Tower of London, Ulyth could not have been more astonished.

"I—!" she stammered. "I—!"

"Yes, you, and you know it. I saw you."

"You couldn't!"

"But I did, or as good as saw you. Who came into our room last night, I should like to know, when Miss Lodge had sent me to bed, and slipped something into one of the blouses hanging behind the door? I'd forgotten by the morning, but I remembered when the pendant came jerking out of my pocket."

"Certainly I didn't put it there!"

"But you did. You came into the room, took off your outdoor coat, and threw it on your bed. I got up, afterwards, and hung it up in your wardrobe for you. Irene told me how you'd joined the cake club. She said you had the password quite pat."

Ulyth was too aghast to answer. Rona, once she had broken silence, continued in a torrent of indignation.

"You a Torch-bearer! You might well ask me not to expose you! 'Remember the Camp-fire,' you said. Yes, it's because of the Camp-fire, and for the sake of the school, that I've kept your secret. Don't be afraid. I'm not going to tell. It wouldn't be good for the League if a Torch-bearer toppled down so low! It doesn't matter so much for only a Wood-gatherer. I won't betray a chum—I've brought that much honour from the Bush; but I'll let you know what I think about you, at any rate."

Then, her blaze of passion suddenly fading, she burst into tears.

"Ulyth, Ulyth, how could you?" she sobbed. "You who taught me everything that was good. I believed in you so utterly, I'd never have thought it of you. Oh, why—"

"Cave! cave!" shouted Lizzie excitedly below. "Cave! Teddie herself!"

Ulyth turned and fled with more regard for speed than safety along the veranda roof, and scrambled through the window into the linen-room again. She was trembling with agitation. Such an extraordinary development of the situation was as appalling as it was unexpected. She must have time to think it over. She could not bear to speak to anybody about it at present, not even to Lizzie. No, she must be alone. She ran quickly downstairs, and, before Lizzie had time to find her, dived under the laurels of the shrubbery and made her way first down the garden and then to the very bottom of the paddock that adjoined the high road. There was a little copse here, of trees and low bushes, which sheltered her from all observation. Nobody was likely to come and disturb her, for the girls preferred the glade, and seldom troubled to enter the paddock. She flung herself down on the grass and tried to face the matter calmly. She had begged Rona to confess, and Rona in return had accused her of taking the pendant. This was turning the tables with a vengeance. How could her room-mate have become possessed of such a preposterous idea? And in what a web of mystery the affair seemed involved! One certainty came as an immense relief. Rona was not guilty. More than this, she was behaving with an extraordinary amount of courage and loyalty.

"She believes I took it, and yet she is bearing all the blame, and shielding me for the sake of the school," groaned Ulyth. "Oh, what must she be thinking of me! We're all at cross-purposes. Did she really fancy that when I said: 'Remember the Camp-fire', I was begging her to screen me? Somebody took the pendant and put it in her pocket; that's the ugly part of the business. It's throwing the blame from one to another. What we've got to do is to find out the real guilty person, and that's not going to be easy, I'm afraid."

Ulyth sighed and wiped her eyes. She had been deeply hurt at Rona's sudden attack. It is humiliating to find that where you occupied a pedestal you are now, even temporarily, a broken idol.

"She's right to scorn me if she imagines I'm such a sneak, but how could she suppose I would? And yet I thought her guilty. Oh dear, it's a horrible muddle! How shall we ever get it straight?"

Ulyth sat thinking, thinking, and was no nearer to a solution of her problem when she suddenly heard the brisk ringing of a bicycle-bell on the road below. Springing up eagerly, she rushed to the wall, and shouted just in time to stop Mrs. Arnold, whose machine was whisking past.

"Hallo, Ulyth! What are you doing there?"

"I'm coming over. Do please wait for me!"

And Ulyth, scrambling somehow across the wall, slid down a gravelly bank on to the road.

"You're the one person in the world I want to see," she added, hugging her friend impetuously. "Oh, Mrs. Arnold, the most dreadful things have been happening at school! Somebody took Stephie's pendant, and it fell out of Rona's pocket, and everybody thinks Rona took it, and Rona thinks it's me. What are we to do?"

"Sit down here and tell me all about it. Yes, please, begin at the very beginning, and don't leave anything out, however trivial. Sometimes the little things are the most important. Cheer up, child! We'll get to the bottom of it, never fear."

Sitting on the bank, with Mrs. Arnold's arm round her, Ulyth related the whole of her story, mentioning every detail she could remember. It was such a comfort to pour it out into sympathetic ears, and to one whose judgment was more likely to be unbiased than that of anyone connected with the school.

"You always understand," she said, with a sigh of relief, as she kissed the hand that was holding hers.

"It certainly is a tangled skein to unravel; but, as it happens, I really believe I can throw a little light upon the matter. You say Rona told you that somebody came into her bedroom last night, and presumably hid the pendant in her blouse pocket?"

"Yes; and she was sure that somebody was myself."

"Then what we have to do is to produce the real culprit."

"If we can find her."

"Just now I was wheeling my bicycle up Tyn y Bryn Hill, and I met one of the boys from Jones's farm. He stopped me and handed me a letter. 'A girl gave it to me five minutes ago,' he said. 'She asked me if I was going to the village, and if I'd post it for her; so I promised I would. But it's addressed to you, so I may as well give it to you as post it, and save the stamp.' I read the letter, and it puzzled me extremely. I hardly knew what to make of it; but since you've told me about the pendant I think I begin to understand its meaning. You shall see it for yourself."

Mrs. Arnold spread out the letter on her knee, so that Ulyth might read it. It was written on village note-paper, in a childish hand, with no stops.

"DEAR MRS ARNOLD

"this comes hoping to find you as well as it leves me at present i am in dredful trubble and i cannot stay here eny longer dear Mrs Arnold after what cook said this afternoon i am sure she knows all and i daresunt tell miss Bowes but you are the camp fire lady and i feel i must say goodbye to ease your mind dear Mrs Arnold wen you get this letter I shall be Far Away as it says in the song you tort us by the stream and you will never see me agen but i shall think of you alwus and the camp fire and i wish i hadn't dun it only I was skared to deth for she said she wuld half kill me and she alwus keeps her wurd your obedient servant Susannah Maude Hawley."

"Susannah Maude!" exclaimed Ulyth. "I never even thought of her. Is it possible that she could have taken the pendant?"

"From the letter it looks rather like it. It is very mysterious, and I cannot understand it all; but the girl appears to have done something she shouldn't, and to have run away."

Angela Brazil

"Where has she run to?"

"She can't have gone very far. She evidently did not mean me to receive this letter until to-morrow morning, as she asked Idwal Jones to post it. He forestalled her intention by giving it to me now. It's a most fortunate thing, as we may be able to overtake her. She is probably walking to Llangarmon, and cannot have gone more than a few miles by this time. I shall follow her at once on my machine, and shall most likely come up with her before she even reaches Coed Glas."

"Oh, let me go with you!" pleaded Ulyth, starting to her feet and seizing the bicycle. "I could ride on the carrier. I've often done it before. Oh, please, please!"

"What about school rules?"

"Miss Bowes wouldn't mind if you took me. Just this once!"

"Well, I suppose my shoulders are broad enough to bear the blame if we get into trouble about it."

"Oh, we shan't! We must find Susannah Maude. Miss Bowes would want us to stop her running away."

"Come along then, and mind you balance yourself, so that you don't upset us."

"Trust me!" chuckled Ulyth delightedly.

Back along the road by which she had come sped Mrs. Arnold, past the lane that led to her own house, and away in the direction of Llangarmon. Ulyth managed to stick on without impeding her progress, and felt a delirious joy in the stolen expedition. To be out with her dear Mrs. Arnold on such an exciting adventure was an hour worth remembering.

She could not often get the Guardian of the Fire all to herself in this glorious fashion. She would be the envy of the school when she returned. Susannah Maude was apparently a quick walker. They passed through the hamlet of Coed Glas, and were half a mile beyond before they caught sight of the odd little figure trudging on ahead. They overtook her exactly on the bridge that crossed the Llyn Mawr stream.

As Mrs. Arnold dismounted and called her by name, Susannah Maude started, uttered a shriek, and apparently for a moment contemplated casting herself into the stream below. The Guardian of the Fire, however, seized her firmly by the arm, and, drawing her to the low parapet, made her sit down.

"Now tell me all about it," said Mrs. Arnold encouragingly, seating herself by her side. For answer Susannah Maude wept unrestrainedly, the hot tears dripping down her hard little cheeks into her rough little hands.

Mrs. Arnold waited with patience till the storm had subsided, then she began to put questions.

"Did you take the young lady's locket, Susan?"

"Yes, I did; but I didn't want to. I wouldn't if I hadn't been so scared. I'm scared to death now as she'll find me."

"You needn't be afraid of Miss Bowes."

"I ain't. Leastways not so bad. It's her I'm feared of."

"Whom do you mean, child?"

"Her—my mother."

"I didn't know you had a mother. I thought you were an orphan," burst out Ulyth.

"I wish I was. No, my father and mother wasn't dead—they was both serving time when I was sent to the Home. When Mother come out she got to know where I was, and she kept an eye on me; then when I comes here to a situation she turns up one day at the back door and says she wants my wages. I give her all I got; but that didn't satisfy her—not much! She was always hanging about the place. She used to come and sell sweets and cakes, unbeknown-like, to the young ladies."

"Was that your mother? The gipsy woman with the basket?" exclaimed Ulyth.

"That was her, sure enough. She pestered me all the time for money, and then when she found I'd got none left she said I must bring her something instead. 'The young ladies must have heaps of brooches and lockets, and things they don't want, so just you fetch me one,' sez she; 'and if you don't I'll catch you and half kill you.' Oh, I can tell you I was scared to death! I don't want not to be honest; but she'd half killed me once or twice before, when I was a kid, and I know what her hand's like when she uses it."

"So you took something?"

"Yes. I waited till the young ladies was all at supper; then I got down one of their coats from the pegs in the corridor and slipped it over my black dress and apron, and I put on one of their hats. I thought if I was seen upstairs they'd take me for one of themselves. I went into the studio, and there, right opposite on a little table, was that kind of locket thing. I slipped it in my pocket, and looked round the room. If there wasn't another just like it on the bench! I took that, and put it on the table. It wasn't likely, perhaps, it would be missed as quick as the other. Then I thought I'd better be going. I was just walking down the landing when I hears a step, and darts into one of the bedrooms. 'Suppose they catches me,' thinks I, 'with one of the young ladies' coats and hats on and the locket in my hand!' There was a blouse hanging behind the door, with a little pocket just handy, so I stuffed the locket down into that; then I pulled off the coat and threw it on the bed, and flung the hat out of the window. I thought if anyone came in and found me I'd say I'd been sent to refill the water-jug. But the steps went on, and I rushed out and downstairs, and left the locket where it was. I was so scared I didn't know what I was doing."

"Gracie found her hat in the garden this morning," gasped Ulyth. "She wondered how it got there."

"But what made you run away?" asked Mrs. Arnold, returning to the main question. "Did you think you were suspected?"

"Not till this afternoon. Then the servants were all talking in the kitchen about how one of the young ladies was supposed to have taken what they called a 'pendon' or something, and Cook looked straight at me and says: 'If anything's missing, it's not one of the young ladies that's got it, I'll be bound.' And I turned red and run out of the kitchen. My mother'd said she'd be coming round this evening, and how was I going to meet her with no locket? So I says, there's nothing else for it, I'd best go back to the Home. Miss Bankes, she was good to me, and Mother daresn't show her face there. So I wrote a letter, and asked Jones's boy to post it. I didn't think you'd get it till to-morrow."

"Very fortunately I received it at once. You must come back with us now to The Woodlands, Susan. We shall all have to walk, for the bicycle won't take three."

"I'll wheel it," cried Ulyth joyfully.

"She'll half kill me to-night," quavered poor Susannah Maude. "Do let me go to the Home!"

"Your mother shall not have a chance of coming near you. You must tell all this to Miss Bowes; then to-morrow, if you wish, you may be sent back to the Orphanage."

No successful scouts could have returned to camp with more triumph than Mrs. Arnold and Ulyth, as, very late and decidedly tired, they arrived at The Woodlands to relate their surprising story. Miss Bowes sent at once for Rona, and in the presence of the Principals the whole matter was carefully explained to the satisfaction of all parties, even poor weeping Susannah Maude.

"I am very glad to find the motive for which Rona kept silence was so good a one," commented Miss Teddington. "She has shown her loyalty both to her friend and to the school."

Dismissed with honour from the study, Ulyth and Rona were hugging each other in the privacy of the boot cupboard.

"Can you ever forgive all the horrible things I said?" implored Rona. "I think I was off my head. I might have known it wasn't—couldn't be possible; you are you—the one girl I've been trying to copy ever since I came here."

"You've quite as much to forgive me, dear, and I beg your pardon. I'm so glad it's all straight and square now."

"You darling! I don't mind telling you it was Tootie who gave me those chocolates."

"Didn't you buy them from the cake-woman?"

"I never bought anything from her. I didn't join the cake club."

"Then how did she get hold of your New Zealand brooch? She showed it to me."

"Why, I'd swopped that brooch with Tootie for a penknife ages ago. We're always swopping our things in IV B."

"The whole business seems to have been a comedy of errors," said Ulyth. "Some mischievous Puck threw dust in our eyes and blinded us to the truth."

After all, it was the juniors that suffered most, for Miss Teddington, who had been very angry at the whole affair, turned the vials of her wrath upon them, and took them to task for their illicit traffic in cakes. This, at any rate, she was determined to punish, and not a solitary sinner was allowed to escape. Tootie, the original leader in rebellion, issued from her interview in the study such a crushed worm as to stifle any lingering seeds of mutiny among her crestfallen followers.

"What's to become of Susannah Maude?" asked everybody; and Miss Bowes answered the question.

"I am taking the poor child back to the Orphanage. I have told the police to warn her disreputable mother from this neighbourhood; but, as one can never be certain when she might turn up again, we must remove Susan altogether out of reach of her evil influence. A party of girls will be sent from the Home very soon to Canada, and we shall arrange for her to join them and emigrate to a new country, where she will be placed in a good situation on a farm and well looked after.

She is not really a dishonest girl, and has a very grateful and affectionate disposition. I am confident that she will do us credit in the New World, and turn out a useful and happy citizen. Why yes, girls, if you like to make her a little good-bye present before she sails, you may do so. It is a kind thought, and I am sure she will appreciate it greatly."

"There's only one item not yet wiped out on the slate," said Ulyth to Lizzie. "Perhaps I ought to report myself for walking along the veranda roof. I'd feel more comfortable!"

"Go ahead, then! Teddie's at the confessional now."

"It's never been exactly forbidden," said Ulyth, with a twinkle in her eye, after she had stated the extent of her enormity to Miss Teddington.

"I would as soon have thought of forbidding you to climb the chimneys! It was a dangerous experiment, and certainly must not be repeated. I'm surprised at a senior! No, as you have told me yourself, I will not enter it in your conduct-book. Please don't parade the roofs in future. Now you may go."

"Got off even easier than I expected," rejoiced Ulyth to the waiting Lizzie. "Teddie's bark's always worse than her bite."

"We've found that out long ago," agreed Lizzie.

CHAPTER XIX

A SURPRISE

The storm-clouds that had gathered round the mystery of the lost pendant seemed to clear the air, and sunshine once more reigned at The Woodlands. The juniors were on their very best behaviour; they indulged in no more surreptitious expeditions and abandoned their truculent attitude towards the elder girls, who, while careful to preserve their dignity as seniors, were ready to wipe off old scores and start afresh. Some manoeuvres in connection with the Camp-fire League proved a bond of union, for here there was no distinction between Upper and Lower School, since all were novices to the new work and had to learn alike. None, indeed, had any time at present to get into mischief. As the end of the term, with its prospects of examinations, drew near, even the most hardened shirkers were obliged to put their shoulders to the wheel, and show a certain amount of intimacy with their textbooks. A nodding acquaintance with French verbs or the rules of Latin Grammar might suffice to shuffle through the ordinary lessons in form, but would be a poor crutch when confronted with a pile of foolscap paper and a set of questions, and likely to lead to disparaging items in their reports.

In every department, therefore, there was a flood-tide of effort. Nature-study diaries, roughly kept, were neatly

Angela Brazil

copied; lists of birds and flowers were revised; the geological specimens in the museum were rearranged and labelled, the art treasures in the studio touched up, while pianos seemed sounding from morning to night. The school was on its mettle to appear at high-water mark. Miss Bowes had lately instituted an Old Girls' Union for The Woodlands, the first gathering of which was to be held in conjunction with the breaking-up festivity. Quite a number of past pupils had accepted the invitation, and people of influence in the neighbourhood were also expected to be present.

"You must show the 'old girls' what you can do," said Miss Bowes, who was naturally anxious to make a good impression on the visitors. "I want them to think the standard raised, not lowered. Some of our ways will be new to them, and we must prove that the changes have been for the better."

It certainly seemed a goal to work for. Even the most irresponsible junior would feel humiliated if the "old girls" were to consider that the school had gone down, and all took a just pride in keeping up its reputation.

"Noelle Derrington and Phyllis Courtenay have accepted"— it was Stephanie who volunteered the information. "They have both been presented. And Irene Vernon has promised to come. She's been out two years now. I do hope those wretched kids in IV B will behave themselves. Manners have gone off at The Woodlands in my opinion, even if the work's better. When my sister was a junior, she says, they would as soon have thought of ragging the mistresses as of cheeking the seniors."

"O tempora! O mores!" laughed Addie. "When you're an old lady, Stephie, you'll spend all your time lamenting the good old days of your youth, and telling the children just how much better-behaved girls used to be when you were at school."

"I shan't say so of our juniors, at any rate," snorted Stephanie.

"Have you heard yet who's coming from the neighbourhood?" Beth enquired.

"Mr. and Mrs. Arnold, of course, and Colonel and Mrs. Hepworth, and the Mowbrays, and the Langtons."

"Lord and Lady Glyncraig have accepted; Miss Harding told me so just now," remarked Christine.

"Oh, what luck!" Stephanie's eyes sparkled. "It will just give the finishing touch to the affair."

"Did you say that Lord and Lady Glyncraig are coming to our breaking-up party?" asked Rona quickly. She had joined the group in company with Winnie and Hattie.

"So I understand; but you needn't excite yourself. It isn't likely they'll notice juniors, though they'll probably speak to a few seniors whom they already know."

"Including Miss Stephanie Radford, of course," scoffed Winnie. "We shall expect to see you walking arm in arm with them round the grounds."

"And hear them giving you a most pressing invitation to Plas Cafn," Hattie added. "You don't get asked there as often as one would suppose, considering you're so intimate with them."

"The cheek of juniors grows beyond all bounds!" declared Stephanie, stalking away. "I'm afraid I know what Irene Vernon will think of the school."

It was of course impossible for all the parents of the girls to come to the "At Home", but a certain proportion had promised to be present. There was a good hotel at Llangarmon, and they could put up there, and drive over for the occasion. The neighbourhood was so beautiful that several would take the opportunity of spending a few days in sightseeing.

"I've news to tell you," said Ulyth to Rona one morning, her face radiant as she showed a letter. "Who do you think are coming to the party? Motherkins and Oswald! Ossie'll just be home in time, so they're jaunting off to Elwyn Bay like a pair of honeymooners. Motherkins hasn't been very well, and Dad says the sea air will do her good—he can't leave business himself, more's the pity! Won't it be glorious to see them here! I could stand on my head, I'm so glad."

The prospect of meeting any members of the Stanton family again was a great pleasure to Rona, who treasured the memory of the Christmas holidays as her happiest experience in England. Mrs. Fowler was also to be present, so she would see the friend who had been kind to her at Eastertide as well.

"I'm glad my mother's coming," said Winnie. "When most of the other girls have somebody, its so horrid to be left out. Poor old Rona! I wish you'd got some relations of your own who could be here. It's hard luck!"

A shade crossed Rona's face. She hesitated, as if about to speak, then, apparently changing her mind, kept silence.

"What an idiotic duffer you are!" whispered Hattie to Winnie. "You needn't be always reminding her what a cuckoo she is."

"The Cuckoo's got its feathers now, and has grown a very

handsome bird," said Winnie, watching Rona as the latter walked away.

The At Home was to be chiefly a gathering for the Old Girls' Union, but the present pupils were to provide a short programme, consisting of music and recitations, to occupy a portion of the afternoon. Only the brightest stars were selected to perform.

"The school's got to show off!" laughed Gertie. "It's to try and take the shine out of the old girls. Miss Bowes doesn't exactly like to say so, but that's what she means."

"No inferior talent permitted," agreed Addie. "Only fresh-water oysters may wag their tails."

"Metaphor's a little mixed, my hearty. Perhaps you'll show us an oyster's tail?"

"Well, they've got beards, at any rate."

"To beard the lion with?"

"If you like. I suppose Lord Glyncraig will be the lion of the afternoon. We shall have to perform before him."

"Oh, I'm so thankful I'm not clever enough to be on the programme!"

After careful consideration of her pupils' best points, Miss Ledbury, the music-mistress, had at last compiled her list. She put Rona down for a song. Rona's voice had developed immensely since she came to school. For a girl of her age it had a wonderfully rich tone and wide compass. Miss Ledbury thought it showed promise of great things later on, and, while avoiding overstraining it, she had made Rona practise most assiduously. There was rather a dearth of good solo voices in the school at present, most of the seniors having more talent for the piano than for singing, otherwise a junior might not have obtained a place on the coveted programme.

"But of course Rona's not exactly a junior," urged Ulyth in reply to several jealous comments. "She's fifteen now, although she's only in IV B, and she's old for her age. She's miles above the kids in her form. I think Teddie realizes that. I shouldn't be at all surprised if Rona skips a form and is put into the Upper School next term. She'd manage the work, I believe. It's been rather rough on her to stay among those babes."

"Well, I say Miss Ledbury might have chosen a soloist from V B," returned Beth icily. She was not a Rona enthusiast.

"Who? Stephie's playing the piano and Gertie's reciting, Merle croaks like a raven, you and Chris don't learn singing, Addie's no ear for tune, and the rest of us, as Leddie says, 'have no puff'. I'm glad Rona can do something well for the school. She's been here three terms, and she's as much a Woodlander now as anyone else."

Rona herself seemed to regard her honour with dismay. The easy confidence which she had brought from New Zealand had quite disappeared, thanks to incessant snubbing; she was apt now to veer to the side of diffidence.

"Do you think I'll break down?" she asked Ulyth nervously.

"Not a bit of it. Why should you? You know the song and you know you can sing it. Just let yourself go, and don't think of the audience."

"Very good advice, no doubt, but a trifle difficult to follow," pouted Rona. "Don't think of the audience, indeed, when they'll all be sitting staring at me. Am I to shut my eyes?"

"You can look at your song, at any rate, and fancy you're alone with Miss Ledbury."

"Imagination's not my strong point. I wish the wretched performance was over and done with."

There were great preparations on the morning of 29th July. Outside, the gardeners were giving a last roll to the lawns, and a last sweep to the paths. In the kitchen the cook was setting out rows of small cakes, and the parlour-maid in the pantry was counting cups and spoons, and polishing the best silver urn. In the school department finishing touches were put everywhere. Great bowls of roses were placed in the drawing-room, and jars of tall lilies in the hall. The studio, arranged yesterday with its exhibits of arts and handicrafts, was further decorated with picturesque boughs of larch and spikes of foxgloves. Two curators were told off to explain the museum to visitors, and tea-stewards selected to help to hand round cups and cakes. A band of special scouts picked raspberries and arranged them on little green plates. Chairs were placed in the summer-house and under the trees in view of the lawn. The rustic seats were carefully dusted in the glade by the stream.

By three o'clock the school was in a flutter of expectation.

"Do I look—decent?" asked Rona anxiously, taking a last nervous peep at her toilet in the wardrobe mirror.

"Decent!" exclaimed Ulyth. "You're for all the world like a Sir Joshua Reynolds portrait. I'd like to frame you, just as you are, and hang you on the wall."

Angela Brazil

"You wouldn't feel ashamed of me if—if you happened to be my relation? I've improved a little since I came here, haven't I? I was a wild sort of goose-girl when I arrived, I know."

"The goose-girl is a Princess to-day," said her room-mate exultantly.

Ulyth thought Rona had never looked so sweet. The pretty white dress trimmed with pale blue edgings suited her exactly, and set off her lovely colouring and rich ruddy-brown hair. Her eyes shone like diamonds, and the mingled excitement and shyness in her face gave a peculiar charm to her expression.

"She's far and away the prettiest girl in the school," reflected Ulyth. "If there were a beauty prize, she'd win it."

Everybody was waiting in the garden when the guests arrived. The scene soon became gay and animated. There were delighted welcomings of parents, enthusiastic meetings between old school chums, and a hearty greeting to all visitors. Mrs. Stanton and Oswald had driven in a taxi from Elwyn Bay, and were received with rapture by Ulyth.

"Motherkins! Oh, how lovely to see you again! I must have you all to myself for just a minute or two before I share you with anybody—even Rona!"

"Is that Rona over there?" asked Oswald, gazing half amazed at the friend who seemed to have added a new dignity to her manner as well as inches to her stature since Christmas-tide.

"Yes, go and fetch her to speak to Motherkins."

"I hardly like to. She looks so stately and grown-up now."

"What nonsense! Ossie, you can't be shy all of a sudden. What's come over you, you silly boy? There, I'll beckon to Rona. Ah, she sees us, and she's coming! No, I'm afraid she can't sit next to us at the concert, because she's one of the performers, and will have to be in the front row."

The ceremonies were to take place in the hall, after which tea would be served to the company out-of-doors.

"Lord Glyncraig is to act as chairman," whispered Addie. "Stephie is so fearfully excited. She means to go and speak to him and Lady Glyncraig afterwards. I hope to goodness they won't have forgotten her. She'd be so woefully humiliated. She wants us all to see that she knows them. She's been just living for this afternoon, I believe."

Rona, her hands tightly clasped, watched the tall figure mount the platform. Lord Glyncraig, with his clear-cut features, iron-grey hair, and commanding air, looked a born leader of men, and well fitted to take his share in swaying a nation's destiny. She could picture him a power in Parliament. It was good of him to come this afternoon to speak at a girls' school. Lady Glyncraig, handsome, well-dressed, and aristocratic, sat in the post of honour next to Miss Bowes. Rona noticed her gracious reception of the beautiful bouquet handed to her by Catherine, and sighed as she looked.

There were no prizes at The Woodlands this year, for the girls had asked to devote the money to the Orphanage; but the examination lists and the annual report were read, and some pleasant comments made upon the scope of the Old Girls' Union. Lord Glyncraig had a happy gift of speech, and could adapt his remarks to the occasion. Everybody felt that he had said exactly the right things, and Principals, mistresses, parents, and pupils past or present were wreathed in smiles. These opening ceremonies did not take very long, and the concert followed immediately.

Marjorie's Prelude, Evie's Nocturne, Stephanie's Mazurka, and Gertie's recitation all went off without a hitch, and received their due reward of appreciation. It was now Rona's turn. For a moment she grew pale as she mounted the platform, then the coral flushed back into her cheeks. She had no time to think of the audience. Miss Ledbury was already playing the opening bars:

"Come out, come out, my dearest dear!
Come out and greet the sun!"

Mellow and tuneful as a blackbird's, Rona's clear rich young voice rang out, so fresh, so joyous, so natural, so full of the very spirit of maying and the glory of summer's return, that the visitors listened as one hearkens to the notes of a bird that is pouring forth its heart from a tree-top in the orchard. There was no mistake about the applause. Guests and girls clapped their hardest. Rona, all unwilling, was recalled, and made to sing an encore, and as she left the platform everybody felt that she had scored the triumph of the occasion.

"Glad the juniors weren't excluded. It's a knock-down for Steph," whispered Addie.

"Trust Miss Ledbury not to leave out Rona. She'll be our champion soloist now," returned Christine.

The rest of the little programme was soon finished, and the audience adjourned to the garden for tea. Stephanie, with a tray of raspberries and cream, came smilingly up to Lord and Lady Glyncraig, and, introducing herself, reminded them of the delightful visit she had paid to Plas Cafn. If they had really forgotten her, they had the good manners not to reveal the fact, and spoke to her kindly and pleasantly.

"By the by," said Lord Glyncraig, "where is your school-fellow who sang so well just now? I don't see her on the lawn."

"Rona Mitchell? I suppose she is somewhere about," replied Stephanie casually.

"Do you happen to know if she comes from New Zealand?"

"Yes, she does."

"I wonder if you could find her and bring her here? I should like very much to speak to her."

Stephanie could not refuse, though her errand was uncongenial. She could not imagine why an ex-Cabinet Minister should concern himself with a girl from the backwoods.

"Lord Glyncraig wants you; so hurry up, and don't keep him waiting," was the message she delivered, not too politely.

Rona blushed furiously. She appeared on the very point of declining to obey the summons.

"Go, dear," said Mrs. Stanton quietly. "Perhaps he wishes to congratulate you on the success of your song. Yes, Rona, go. It would be most ungracious to refuse."

With a face in which shyness, nervousness, pride, and defiance strove for the mastery, Rona approached Lord Glyncraig. He held out his hand to her.

"Won't you bury the hatchet, and let us be friends at last,

Rona?" he said. "I'm proud of my granddaughter to-day. You're a true chip of the old block, a Mitchell to your finger-tips—and" (in a lower tone) "with your mother's voice thrown into the bargain. Blood is thicker than water, child, and it's time now for bygones to become bygones. I shall write to your father to-night, and set things straight."

*   *   *   *   *

"How is it that you've actually been a whole year at The Woodlands and never let anybody have the least hint that Lord Glyncraig is your grandfather? Don't you know what an enormous difference it would have made to your position in the school? Stephie is quite hysterical about it. Why was it such a dead secret?" asked Ulyth of her room-mate, as they took off their party dresses, when the guests had gone.

"It's rather a long story," replied Rona, sitting down on her bed. "In the first place, I dare say you've guessed that Dad was the prodigal of the family. He never did anything very bad, poor dear, but he was packed off to the colonies in disgrace, and told that he might stay there. At Melbourne he met a lovely opera singer, who was on tour in Australia, and married her. That made my grandfather more angry than anything else he had done. I'm not ashamed of my mother. She was very clever, and sang like an angel, I'm told, though I can't remember her. When she died, Dad went to New Zealand and started farming. Mrs. Barker was hardly an ideal person to bring me up, but she was the only woman we could get to stop in such an out-of-the-way place. I must have been an awful specimen of a child; I don't like to remember what things I did then. When I was about ten, Father went away for a few weeks to the North Island, and while he was gone, Mrs. Barker went off in the gig to have a day's shopping at the nearest store. She left me alone in the house. I wasn't frightened, for I was quite accustomed to it. No one but a chance neighbour ever came near. Yet that day was just the exception that proves the rule. Early in the afternoon a grand travelling motor drove up, and a lady and gentleman knocked at the door, and enquired for Dad. I was a little wild rough thing then, and I was simply scared to death at the sight of strangers. I told them Dad was away. Then they asked if they might come in, and the gentleman said he was my grandfather, and the lady was his new wife, so that she was my step-grandmother. Now Mrs. Barker had always rubbed it in to me that if I was left alone I must on no account admit strangers. That was the only thing I could think of. I was in a panic, and I slammed the door on them and bolted it, and then ran to the window and pulled faces, hoping to make them go away. They stood for a minute or two quite aghast, trying to get me to listen to reason through the window, but I only grew more and more frightened, and called them all the ugly names I could.

"'It's no use attempting to tame such a young savage,' said the lady at last. Then they got into their car again and drove away.

"By the time Mrs. Barker arrived I was ashamed of myself, so I said nothing about my adventure, and I never dared to tell Dad a word of it. I suppose his father had come to hunt him up; but he was evidently discouraged at the reception he had received at the farm, and went back to England without making another attempt at a meeting. I don't believe he and Dad ever wrote to each other from year's end to year's end. I tried to forget this, but it stuck in my memory all the same. Time went by, my friendship with you began, and it was decided that I should be sent to The Woodlands. I knew my grandfather lived at Plas Cafn, for Dad had told me about his old home, but I did not know it was so near to the school. You ask why I did not tell the girls that I was related to Lord Glyncraig? There were several reasons. In the first place, I was really very much ashamed of my behaviour the day he had come to our farm. I thought he had cast us off completely, and would not be at all pleased to own me as granddaughter. I would not confess it to any of you, but I felt so rough and uncouth when I compared myself with other girls that I did not want Lord Glyncraig to see me, or to know that I was in the neighbourhood. Perhaps some day, so I thought, I might grow more like you, if I tried hard, and then it would be time enough to tell him of my whereabouts. Then, because he had disowned us, I felt much too proud to boast about the relationship at school. If you could not like me for myself, I wouldn't make a bid for popularity on the cheap basis of being his granddaughter. I'm a democrat at heart, and I think people ought to be valued on their own merits entirely. I'd rather be an outsider than shine with a reflected glory."

"You'll be popular now," said Ulyth. "Are you to spend the holidays at Plas Cafn?"

"Yes. Miss Bowes says I must, though I'd far rather have accepted your invitation. Lady Glyncraig was very kind and sweet; she kissed me and said she hoped so much that we should be friends. They have promised to ask Dad to come over for next Christmas and have a big family reunion."

"You won't let them take you away from The Woodlands? We don't want to lose you, dear. You must stay here now—for the sake of the school."

"For my own sake!" cried Rona, flinging her arms round her friend. "Ulyth, I owe everything in the world to you. I understand now how good it was of you to take me into your room and teach me. I was a veritable cuckoo in your nest then, a horrid, tiresome, trespassing bird, a savage, a bear cub, a 'backwoods gawk' as the girls called me. It's entirely thanks to you if at last I'm—"

"The sweetest Prairie Rose that ever came out of the wilderness!" finished Ulyth warmly.

Choose from Thousands of 1stWorldLibrary Classics By

A. M. Barnard
Ada Leverson
Adolphus William Ward
Aesop
Agatha Christie
Alexander Aaronsohn
Alexander Kielland
Alexandre Dumas
Alfred Gatty
Alfred Ollivant
Alice Duer Miller
Alice Turner Curtis
Alice Dunbar
Allen Chapman
Alleyne Ireland
Ambrose Bierce
Amelia E. Barr
Amory H. Bradford
Andrew Lang
Andrew McFarland Davis
Andy Adams
Angela Brazil
Anna Alice Chapin
Anna Sewell
Annie Besant
Annie Hamilton Donnell
Annie Payson Call
Annie Roe Carr
Annonaymous
Anton Chekhov
Archibald Lee Fletcher
Arnold Bennett
Arthur C. Benson
Arthur Conan Doyle
Arthur M. Winfield
Arthur Ransome
Arthur Schnitzler
Arthur Train
Atticus
B.H. Baden-Powell
B. M. Bower
B. C. Chatterjee
Baroness Emmuska Orczy
Baroness Orczy
Basil King
Bayard Taylor
Ben Macomber
Bertha Muzzy Bower
Bjornstjerne Bjornson

Booth Tarkington
Boyd Cable
Bram Stoker
C. Collodi
C. E. Orr
C. M. Ingleby
Carolyn Wells
Catherine Parr Traill
Charles A. Eastman
Charles Amory Beach
Charles Dickens
Charles Dudley Warner
Charles Farrar Browne
Charles Ives
Charles Kingsley
Charles Klein
Charles Hanson Towne
Charles Lathrop Pack
Charles Romyn Dake
Charles Whibley
Charles Willing Beale
Charlotte M. Braeme
Charlotte M. Yonge
Charlotte Perkins Stetson
Clair W. Hayes
Clarence Day Jr.
Clarence E. Mulford
Clemence Housman
Confucius
Coningsby Dawson
Cornelis DeWitt Wilcox
Cyril Burleigh
D. H. Lawrence
Daniel Defoe
David Garnett
Dinah Craik
Don Carlos Janes
Donald Keyhoe
Dorothy Kilner
Dougan Clark
Douglas Fairbanks
E. Nesbit
E. P. Roe
E. Phillips Oppenheim
E. S. Brooks
Earl Barnes
Edgar Rice Burroughs
Edith Van Dyne
Edith Wharton

Edward Everett Hale
Edward J. O'Biren
Edward S. Ellis
Edwin L. Arnold
Eleanor Atkins
Eleanor Hallowell Abbott
Eliot Gregory
Elizabeth Gaskell
Elizabeth McCracken
Elizabeth Von Arnim
Ellem Key
Emerson Hough
Emilie F. Carlen
Emily Bronte
Emily Dickinson
Enid Bagnold
Enilor Macartney Lane
Erasmus W. Jones
Ernie Howard Pie
Ethel May Dell
Ethel Turner
Ethel Watts Mumford
Eugene Sue
Eugenie Foa
Eugene Wood
Eustace Hale Ball
Evelyn Everett-green
Everard Cotes
F. H. Cheley
F. J. Cross
F. Marion Crawford
Fannie E. Newberry
Federick Austin Ogg
Ferdinand Ossendowski
Fergus Hume
Florence A. Kilpatrick
Fremont B. Deering
Francis Bacon
Francis Darwin
Frances Hodgson Burnett
Frances Parkinson Keyes
Frank Gee Patchin
Frank Harris
Frank Jewett Mather
Frank L. Packard
Frank V. Webster
Frederic Stewart Isham
Frederick Trevor Hill
Frederick Winslow Taylor

Friedrich Kerst
Friedrich Nietzsche
Fyodor Dostoyevsky
G.A. Henty
G.K. Chesterton
Gabrielle E. Jackson
Garrett P. Serviss
Gaston Leroux
George A. Warren
George Ade
Geroge Bernard Shaw
George Cary Eggleston
George Durston
George Ebers
George Eliot
George Gissing
George MacDonald
George Meredith
George Orwell
George Sylvester Viereck
George Tucker
George W. Cable
George Wharton James
Gertrude Atherton
Gordon Casserly
Grace E. King
Grace Gallatin
Grace Greenwood
Grant Allen
Guillermo A. Sherwell
Gulielma Zollinger
Gustav Flaubert
H. A. Cody
H. B. Irving
H.C. Bailey
H. G. Wells
H. H. Munro
H. Irving Hancock
H. R. Naylor
H. Rider Haggard
H. W. C. Davis
Haldeman Julius
Hall Caine
Hamilton Wright Mabie
Hans Christian Andersen
Harold Avery
Harold McGrath
Harriet Beecher Stowe
Harry Castlemon
Harry Coghill
Harry Houidini

Hayden Carruth
Helent Hunt Jackson
Helen Nicolay
Hendrik Conscience
Hendy David Thoreau
Henri Barbusse
Henrik Ibsen
Henry Adams
Henry Ford
Henry Frost
Henry James
Henry Jones Ford
Henry Seton Merriman
Henry W Longfellow
Herbert A. Giles
Herbert Carter
Herbert N. Casson
Herman Hesse
Hildegard G. Frey
Homer
Honore De Balzac
Horace B. Day
Horace Walpole
Horatio Alger Jr.
Howard Pyle
Howard R. Garis
Hugh Lofting
Hugh Walpole
Humphry Ward
Ian Maclaren
Inez Haynes Gillmore
Irving Bacheller
Isabel Cecilia Williams
Isabel Hornibrook
Israel Abrahams
Ivan Turgenev
J.G.Austin
J. Henri Fabre
J. M. Barrie
J. M. Walsh
J. Macdonald Oxley
J. R. Miller
J. S. Fletcher
J. S. Knowles
J. Storer Clouston
J. W. Duffield
Jack London
Jacob Abbott
James Allen
James Andrews
James Baldwin

James Branch Cabell
James DeMille
James Joyce
James Lane Allen
James Lane Allen
James Oliver Curwood
James Oppenheim
James Otis
James R. Driscoll
Jane Abbott
Jane Austen
Jane L. Stewart
Janet Aldridge
Jens Peter Jacobsen
Jerome K. Jerome
Jessie Graham Flower
John Buchan
John Burroughs
John Cournos
John F. Kennedy
John Gay
John Glasworthy
John Habberton
John Joy Bell
John Kendrick Bangs
John Milton
John Philip Sousa
John Taintor Foote
Jonas Lauritz Idemil Lie
Jonathan Swift
Joseph A. Altsheler
Joseph Carey
Joseph Conrad
Joseph E. Badger Jr
Joseph Hergesheimer
Joseph Jacobs
Jules Vernes
Julian Hawthrone
Julie A Lippmann
Justin Huntly McCarthy
Kakuzo Okakura
Karle Wilson Baker
Kate Chopin
Kenneth Grahame
Kenneth McGaffey
Kate Langley Bosher
Kate Langley Bosher
Katherine Cecil Thurston
Katherine Stokes
L. A. Abbot
L. T. Meade

L. Frank Baum
Latta Griswold
Laura Dent Crane
Laura Lee Hope
Laurence Housman
Lawrence Beasley
Leo Tolstoy
Leonid Andreyev
Lewis Carroll
Lewis Sperry Chafer
Lilian Bell
Lloyd Osbourne
Louis Hughes
Louis Joseph Vance
Louis Tracy
Louisa May Alcott
Lucy Fitch Perkins
Lucy Maud Montgomery
Luther Benson
Lydia Miller Middleton
Lyndon Orr
M. Corvus
M. H. Adams
Margaret E. Sangster
Margret Howth
Margaret Vandercook
Margaret W. Hungerford
Margret Penrose
Maria Edgeworth
Maria Thompson Daviess
Mariano Azuela
Marion Polk Angellotti
Mark Overton
Mark Twain
Mary Austin
Mary Catherine Crowley
Mary Cole
Mary Hastings Bradley
Mary Roberts Rinehart
Mary Rowlandson
M. Wollstonecraft Shelley
Maud Lindsay
Max Beerbohm
Myra Kelly
Nathaniel Hawthrone
Nicolo Machiavelli
O. F. Walton
Oscar Wilde

Owen Johnson
P.G. Wodehouse
Paul and Mabel Thorne
Paul G. Tomlinson
Paul Severing
Percy Brebner
Percy Keese Fitzhugh
Peter B. Kyne
Plato
Quincy Allen
R. Derby Holmes
R. L. Stevenson
R. S. Ball
Rabindranath Tagore
Rahul Alvares
Ralph Bonehill
Ralph Henry Barbour
Ralph Victor
Ralph Waldo Emmerson
Rene Descartes
Ray Cummings
Rex Beach
Rex E. Beach
Richard Harding Davis
Richard Jefferies
Richard Le Gallienne
Robert Barr
Robert Frost
Robert Gordon Anderson
Robert L. Drake
Robert Lansing
Robert Lynd
Robert Michael Ballantyne
Robert W. Chambers
Rosa Nouchette Carey
Rudyard Kipling
Saint Augustine
Samuel B. Allison
Samuel Hopkins Adams
Sarah Bernhardt
Sarah C. Hallowell
Selma Lagerlof
Sherwood Anderson
Sigmund Freud
Standish O'Grady
Stanley Weyman
Stella Benson
Stella M. Francis

Stephen Crane
Stewart Edward White
Stijn Streuvels
Swami Abhedananda
Swami Parmananda
T. S. Ackland
T. S. Arthur
The Princess Der Ling
Thomas A. Janvier
Thomas A Kempis
Thomas Anderton
Thomas Bailey Aldrich
Thomas Bulfinch
Thomas De Quincey
Thomas Dixon
Thomas H. Huxley
Thomas Hardy
Thomas More
Thornton W. Burgess
U. S. Grant
Upton Sinclair
Valentine Williams
Various Authors
Vaughan Kester
Victor Appleton
Victor G. Durham
Victoria Cross
Virginia Woolf
Wadsworth Camp
Walter Camp
Walter Scott
Washington Irving
Wilbur Lawton
Wilkie Collins
Willa Cather
Willard F. Baker
William Dean Howells
William le Queux
W. Makepeace Thackeray
William W. Walter
William Shakespeare
Winston Churchill
Yei Theodora Ozaki
Yogi Ramacharaka
Young E. Allison
Zane Grey

www.ingramcontent.com/pod-product-compliance
Lightning Source LLC
Chambersburg PA
CBHW050030180626
46810CB00002B/657